THE WELL IS DEEP

Prayers to Draw Up Living Water

∞

Virginia Ric

UNITED CHURCH PRESS
Cleveland, Ohio

United Church Press, Cleveland, Ohio 44115
© 1999 by Virginia Rickeman

Biblical quotations are from the New Revised Standard Version of the Bible,
© 1989 by the Division of Christian Education of the National Council of the
Churches of Christ in the U.S.A., and are used by permission

Printed in the United States of America on acid-free paper

04 03 02 01 00 99 5 4 3 2 1

Library of Congress Cataloging-in-Publication Data
Rickeman, Virginia.
    The well is deep : prayers to draw up living water / Virginia Rickeman.
        p. cm.
    ISBN 0-8298-1325-X (pbk. : alk. paper)
    1. Prayers. 2. Church year—Prayer—books and devotions—English.
    I. Title.
  BV245.R56 1999
  242'.8058—dc21   98-50327
                                                               CIP

To the people of
Plymouth Congregational Church,
Minneapolis, Minnesota,
for whom and with whom these prayers were first written

· CONTENTS ·

· PREFACE ·

Although I have presumed to call the passages printed in this book "prayers," words actually become prayers only as people pray them. Of course, it is also possible to pray without words. One may, for example, pray through dancing, making music, contemplating an icon, or, as the apostle Paul wrote, "with sighs too deep for words" (Romans 8:26). Nevertheless, many of us continue to find words extremely helpful to praying.

Words do not always come easily, however. Particularly when we are asked to pray with other people, many of us feel tongue-tied. Nor does solitude necessarily make praying easier; we often wonder where or how to begin. My hope is that the words in this book will function as ropes to help you lower heart, mind, and spirit into the deep, inexhaustible well of God's Spirit in order to draw up living water for yourself and to share with others.

Many thanks are due to the members, staff, and ordained colleagues of Plymouth Congregational Church in Minneapolis with whom I have the wonderful opportunity to minister. Special thanks go to Joyce Malmquist for her typing skills and all-round dependability.

PRAYERS FOR THE CHURCH YEAR

· ADVENT ·

Ambivalence

God, merciful God, we are entering our season of ambivalence. Twinkling lights, pungent pine boughs, the strains of familiar music kindle feelings of warmth and excitement. At the same time, the lengthening nights and deepening cold tug our spirits toward gloom. The church's liturgy speaks of waiting. Yet all too often we find there is too much to do to leave time for waiting, while a weariness of body and soul makes any attempt to stay awake laughable. We look for the promised peace and goodwill, but our ears are assailed with stories of war overseas and the invective of talk-show hosts at home.

We are torn in two, O God: full of resignation and hope, comfort and dread, desperate to understand and desperately uncertain what it all means. Above all, we are filled with longing:

- Longing for contentment and a sense of purpose
- Aching for relief from old wounds and griefs
- Nostalgia for the simplicity and homeyness of childhood
- Yearning for everything somehow to turn out all right in the end in spite of ourselves
- Longing for renewed and better selves

God, help us turn all the hungers of our hearts to you. We look into each others' eyes, into the faces of our children, and realize that you have not given up on us. In sudden shock we understand that your longing is even greater than ours. Nothing will stop your coming to be with us, bringing fresh courage and a fiercer commitment to the ways of love. Amen.

From the Dark

In the times of darkness, O God, we so easily become confused. We mistake control for power, and need for love. Thank you for not despairing of us. Thank you for persistently drawing us toward the light of wisdom and goodness. So shall gladness fill our souls and even the shadows dance for joy. Come, O sun of righteousness; dawn in us today. Amen.

If We Could

God, we would make a highway for you through the wilderness of our lives. We would cut through the thicket of our busy hours, lever aside the boulders of shame and fear, fill in the potholes of boredom, mend the eroded gullies of grief, level the frost heaves of anger and hate. Yes, God, it would please us to be able to build a road to bring you to us, but somehow we keep failing to even half complete it. What are we lacking? What are we forgetting? Why is it so difficult to clear a way for you?

And a voice whispers, "Hush. Be still. Wait."

God, we would have our lives mean something. We would do our part to make the world a kinder, happier, more beautiful place. We would soothe another's hurt, feed another's hunger, pull down walls and open doors. We would work to be instruments of your justice and peace, God. Yet there is just so much time in each day and there are the practical matters of car repairs and dentist appointments; returning phone calls, writing reports, meeting clients; shoveling the front walk, doing laundry, eating, sleeping. Are these merely lame excuses? Do you expect more and better from us as citizens of your commonwealth? How can we possibly . . . ?

And a voice says, "Quiet. Listen. Wait."

God, we would be properly grateful for all the blessings in our lives. We would count up all the love and health and material comfort that is ours and pour out glad thanks to you. But then we look at the unloved or the ill or the poor and grow uneasy. How can we be joyful in our gratitude when others are without? Are these gifts of chance rather than evidence of your loving-kindness? Are we grateful for the wrong things? What sort of thanksgiving is acceptable to you?

And a voice cries, "Silence! Watch! Wait!"

Ah, God, it is not up to us. You and you alone are God. You are the one who topples mountains and raises up valleys. You are the one who creates, renews, and transforms. We do not build for you; you build for us. Weak, vulnerable, humble ones are your people of choice. Can we learn, for your sake, for our sakes, to be so meek? We have only clever minds, stubborn hearts, and strong wills to give you, God. And we may be giving them oh, so tentatively, until that dawn when we, together with all people, shall see your glory revealed. Take our silence, our watchfulness, our waiting as our praise to you. Amen.

Island of Calm

It is good to be here, God. Thank you for this island of calm in the turbulent stream of Christmas preparations. We are grateful that your coming to us is independent of lights and presents, ribbons and wrapping, cards and cookies. You arrive to make yourself at home in whatever lowly space we have not yet filled with work, duty, pleasure, or sleep. Come, Emmanuel, that we may come home, too. Amen.

Memories

God of our days and seasons, how the lights and sounds and scents of December call up the memories buried deep within us: memories of childhood anticipation and pleasures; remembrances of friends and family members with endearing peculiarities, special talents, and distinctive tastes; thoughts of kitchens and front parlors, store windows and mail-order catalogs; memories we wrap around ourselves like blankets. Thank you, God, for the gift of remembering.

Help us, God, to cherish our histories without so overindulging in nostalgia that we neglect the wonder of the present moment. Grant us the insight and wisdom to create for others small surprises of beauty and warmth that bring to both us and them the double pleasure of happiness now and glowing memories for the future. Awaken us to the many gifts all around us, ours for the seizing with eye and nose and ear, to savor and share.

We pray for our children. The power we have to shape their memories is an awesome responsibility, God. Guide us as we seek to instill in them foundations of trust, hope, love, and joy that will uphold them in their living and growing. We would teach them generosity by being generous ourselves, service by serving others ourselves, and faith by faithful living ourselves, but we know how much we need your help to do this. As they develop, lead us to an awareness and appreciation of each one's unique offering of creativity, humor, vision, strength, or compassion. As we attempt to hand on to them the traditions we value and the stories that have formed us, may we also learn from our children and be open to the stories they have to tell us.

Then we will together own the common memory of your great love and how you once came to us in the guise of an infant. All praise and thanks to you, O God, then and now and forevermore. Amen.

Promise of Peace

God, we who have lived through many an Advent season recognize an old ache. Every year, about this time, we feel again a familiar poignancy, a dull pang, a hollow, wistful longing for the peace of Christmas.

We see the muddle, the sadness, the anxiety in our hearts and long for peace at our centers—a gracious serenity, a depth of stillness. If we possessed such calm, then we could ride out life's storms, we could control our fears, we would be strong and truly compassionate. Is this the Christmas peace you promise?

We look at the anger, pain, and emptiness in relationships and ache for peace with those we live and work beside—a mutual respect, a shared appreciation, a loyal trust. If we felt such goodwill, then we could risk speaking the truth, then we could forgive and seek forgiveness, then our love would bear sweet, full-rounded fruit. Do you promise us this peace someday?

God, we listen to the news and sigh for peace among peoples—between Tutsi and Hutu, Serb and Croat, Israeli and Arab, American and Iraqi. If all weapons were destroyed, if everyone would speak with civility and act with forbearance, then we could turn our focus fully on ensuring justice, creating beauty, improving life for everyone. Is *this* the Christmas peace you promise someday?

O God, we hunger for peace on earth, for peace throughout the world, among all species and spirits, energies and elements, from pole to pole, from earth's core to its heavens. We yearn for the complete, whole goodness you had in mind when you began creating. Do you still promise such peace someday? How long must we wait? Why, after all these centuries since Christ's birth, does it seem as distant, as improbable as ever?

We know that we have, individually, failed to cultivate peace as diligently as we might have. Yet the world's turmoil and violence seem to be bigger, beyond, far more than any personal failure. You, God, only you have the power and wisdom to reorder our lives and relationships, our institutions and systems.

But all you promise is Christmas peace: a baby whose power is utter vulnerability, a baby who is totally lacking in any worldly wisdom. How can such a one save us? If this is all you promise, God, how can we continue to hope? Yet what other choice do we have but to trust you?

God, hear our prayers for peace. Hear our silent tears and our brave, foolish hopes. Hear us for the sake of our children and our small, beautiful earthly home. Hear, O God, and grant us your peace that surpasses all our understanding. Amen.

The Realm to Be
(ISAIAH 11:6–9)

Help us, God, to imagine a realm where rich lie down with poor; healthy with ill; Christian, Jew, and Muslim together. The wicked and the virtuous share a meal, the complacent and the suffering hold hands, and a little child is leading them. Help us, God, to hunger for this realm where love rules, where both the forgiving and the forgiven know themselves blessed, where nothing separates us from you. Let heaven and earth be one in reflecting your glory. Amen.

The Refiner
(MALACHI 3:1–4)

Blazing God, we pray to you for light and warmth. Burn off the haze of confusion and temper the cold of indifference. Yet we tremble lest you come too close. We want only a small flame, just a portion of your Spirit, merely a fraction of your power. We fear you will melt us down with a love so fiercely tender that we will be changed beyond recognition. If you refine us with your holy fire, will you then plunge us into deep, wet joy? Amen.

· CHRISTMAS ·

Christmas Eve

God, in the midst of wondering doubt and faithful hope you come to us. With dark and quiet grace you bring to birth a love beyond our deserving, and peace beyond our understanding. Let the glad tidings resound: you are with us. We know not how, but mystery has been given form, and wisdom has come to life in a human birth. Flesh has become sacred; touch, holy. Tonight with the angels we cry out, "Glory!" for with Christ we have become new and full and joyous again. Amen.

Christmas Light

God, help us to view past, present, and future by the light of Christmas. Then we can value peace, but not at the expense of injustice. We will treasure comfort and safety, but not by excluding those who have neither. We will measure our success by the smiles on children's faces and our wisdom by the serenity in their eyes. So may Christ find welcome in our hearts and homes. Amen.

Unexpected

God, we wonder again at the ways you choose to come to us: not in wind, earthquake, or fire, but in the sound of sheer silence. Not with armies, processions, or shows of splendor, but as an ordinary baby in a poor, dark stable. We do not quite comprehend how storm and song can be contained in stillness. We do not yet understand how power and might can be clothed in fragile flesh. But we come today with our half hopes, our little faiths, our hungry hearts to meet you. Ah, God, you are not what we expected. Amen.

· EPIPHANY ·

Divine Infant

God of bright mystery, when your power and your glory leave us dazzled and confused, help us to remember your entering the world as a baby. You came skin soft and human scented. You spoke only the language of tears. You knew simply hunger and food, cold and warmth, the goodness of a sweet, low song and a tender touch. Even now, the riches of kings mean nothing. You cry for our love as a baby cries for milk. Amen.

Light in Winter

Wondrous God, we give you thanks for winter light:

For the early morning brightening from pearl to rose to gold
    that awakens us, body and spirit;

For the warm-cold dayshine of sun and sky and snow that
    puts smiles on faces and a bounce in each step;

For the low, blushing, sideways glance of twilight that calls us
    home;

For all the lamp-lit rooms that draw us in;

For fat moon whiteness that keeps watch high above the living
    night;

For all such energy and beauty, God, we give you glad praise.

Thank you, too, for all the qualities of life we name by
    metaphors of light:

For learning, reason, and understanding;

For purity and goodness, wisdom, truth, and hope;

For the realm of heaven where your will is done and your
    glory revealed;

For all that brings illumination to our lives and our world, we
    offer deep gratitude to you, O God.

We know that these qualities come to us in varied ways, but chiefly through the words and deeds of other people. Therefore, we ask your blessing on the kinfolk and teachers, the friends and healers, the artists, authors, coaches, and leaders who have been sources of light for us. Amen.

Shining through the Cracks

O God, there are corners of our lives and corners of our world that appear to be bereft of light. We pray that your shining presence glow more strongly through the cracks that we may more readily affirm that there is no place within or beyond us that you have abandoned. May we see more clearly your promise to make us bearers of light. Help us to understand how we can be most faithful to the tasks you set before us. We pray that you use our weaknesses as well as our strengths, our failures as well as our successes, to bring love and truth to light. Give us the will and the courage to act with honesty and generosity even when it might cost us embarrassment or inconvenience. Remind us that we are neither as important nor as insignificant as we are sometimes tempted to believe.

And whatever the present radiance of our lives, this is how we know that you love us still: you continually create new and surprising ways to reveal your true self to us. Only grant us the faith to live through our unseeing times, trusting that, in the end, even death is not strong enough to extinguish the light of your love. Amen.

Paradox

God, we experience your love as we experience light: with wonder, gratitude, and bewilderment. Your love meets us in dazzling paradox, like particles scattered around our shadowy selves, like waves washing the shores of our stony hearts. In all directions your love radiates, like sunlight into far space: ceaseless and continuous, without measure or calculation, untimed, independent of our perception or response. Yet, as a singular laser beam you focus particular love into each created being in precise quantities to excite, to energize, to dance with the electrons of life.

Beyond our understanding and control, your love delights us with its beauty, confounds us with its playfulness, frightens us with its clarity.

God, what if your love reveals what we do not wish to see? What if your love lures us down roads toward unknown lands? What if your love waxes fierce, destroying things we cherish? What if your love burns out?

We find it easier to trust the steadiness of the sun, for all its stormy flares, than the power of your love. We think it easier to maintain control by letting in just a little light, just a little of your love—not enough to disrupt comfortable routines; not enough to derail rational, ordered plans; not enough to change anything, least of all ourselves.

When, God, in your mercy, our contrivances fail, we may be puzzled. We thought we were following the rules. We thought we were being dutiful and good. We thought we had a bargain with you. We may be angry. What have we done to deserve suffering, pain, loss, death? Isn't this what your love is supposed to shield us from? And sometimes, God, we are grateful. We see all the anxious time and energy and creativity we used up trying to manipulate your love. We are glad to lay down our sandbagged certainties in exchange for winged faith. We smile at how foolish we have been to hope for so little from you, to expect so little of ourselves.

Thank you, God, for piercing our souls with the light of your love, for drowning us in a love radiant with all the colors we know and don't know. Thank you for assaulting us with a glory so luminous, so tender, that all our defenses against you crumble and we succumb to awe.

What love is this that judges all and condemns none?
That is complete in itself and yearns for us?
That empties itself of power and conquers all evil?
That is silent as light and answers every cry?
That is divinity itself and wrapped in flesh?

Praise to you, O God of lightning love. Praise to you for holy paradox. Amen.

· LENT ·

Living on Faith

God, sometimes it is frightening to live on faith alone. We would much rather feel your presence, reason out your will, witness a miracle, or rely on someone else who is more certain of your voice. But, you say, Lent is a time of absence, uncertainty, barren desert, and loneliness. In Lent you confront us with our worst fears and no reassurances, only the demand to live on faith.

God, we thought that was for holy, called-apart saints. Our own faith isn't that special or that strong. What do you mean, Not *yet*? Wait a minute, God. We aren't ready for this way of building faith. It's confusing. It hurts. It's terrifying. Where are you? Why have you left us like this? Don't turn away from us. We need you. Our world needs you. Aren't you going to do something about all the voices oozing hatred? Don't you care about all the self-centeredness and greed? Look at the violence, God, in homes and streets and minefields. Hear the cries of hurting children and the sobs of grieving parents. Do not abandon us to these treacherous forces around us, among us, within us. You cannot mean that this is our wilderness to journey through. We'll die!

O God, we do not want to die. Even when we know in our heads that old ways must die for the new to be born, we are not willing to let go our hold on the old. It's all we have, God. Surely you understand?

Yes, faith tells us this much: you understand. And if you hide yourself from us for a time—for, say, forty days—we will wait. You have yourself called us a stiff-necked people. So, all right, we will stubbornly wait. We may yet die, but we'll wait. If we cannot feel or know or see or hear you, still we can wait. Maybe waiting is all the faith we need for now. So be it. We will set our teeth, grimace, and wait. In silence we will wait for the movement of your Spirit.

And in waiting, God, we remember. We remember that your Spirit is like breath, softly rising and falling within us and in spite of all we otherwise feel or know or do. We remember that your Spirit is like wind, sometimes silent, causing ascending columns of smoke to barely quiver, sometimes roaring through the treetops with a power that awes us. We remember that your Spirit moves as you will, whether or not we or they or anyone is awake or aware, whether or not anyone is ready. And that is enough.

Therefore, O God, we will live on faith as we can and by your grace when faith fails us, this day and all the days of our living and dying and journeying toward new life in you. Amen.

Into the Wilderness

Toward what wilderness, God, are you leading us?

Into what wasteland—dangerous, barren, devilish, and empty—would you draw us?

Do you press us toward the city outside these doors? Into streets indifferent to suffering, through buildings that shelter despair, down alleys that deal in rage? How shall we answer the taunts, "If you are Christians, give us money, give us bread"? Will we feel tempted to assuage a gnawing guilt with some token loaf?

We have your word that bread alone will not bring life either to us or to those we name "poor." Life—warm, crusty, chewy, fragrant life. How our mouths water for it, God! Come, feed us all here together with your rich, abundant goodness. Feed us by each others' hands.

Or is the dry desert of the secular worldview the wilderness into which you prod us? The vast reaches of power; blazing fame; subtle, shifting, golden sands of authority shimmer before us. You know our weakness, God. You know our temptation to look for both security and freedom in wealth or insurance policies; in weapons and armed forces; in strength, control, connections, and strategic alliances.

The desert is so beguiling, God; only gradually does each oasis have a way of turning into another mirage. Is this all there is? We cannot long worship such sere, severe majesty before we die of thirst. We must turn to you and look to you alone to keep us. Well up within us, Holy Spirit, clear, cool, stone-deep; well up within us until we overflow with your life-giving joy.

Or, God, are you drawing us down into an inner wilderness where canyons of doubt are crisscrossed with gullies of loss and shame? Where shadows deepen early and stay late and we are no longer sure what is true or real or even who we are? Terror lurks in these badlands, where we wander lost, alone, or— worse—dogged by nameless ghosts.

We would conjure your presence, God, with some ritual; some magical prayer; some secret, sure incantation that would assure us of our special place in your heart. But you retreat into the darkness while rock walls all around reverberate with a silent, single word, "Trust."

We are here, God, on the brink of whatever Lenten wilderness is ours to walk through now. We are here together, uneasy, uncertain, maybe even unwilling. Yet, by your grace, we are here. Spirit of Christ, lead us as you will. Amen.

A Fearsome Thing

It is a fearsome thing to fall into your hands, holy and mysterious God, for we do not know when you will choose to comfort us or when to disturb us. If our lives are in upheaval and we long for resolution, you do not always rescue us from the tumult, but whisper, "Trust me." When chronic pain or anxiety wearies us by day and keeps us awake by night, your voice speaks from the darkness, saying only, "I am here. I will bear you up. Lean on me." When our minds are perplexed and our emotions confused, we often hear but the one word "Wait." Worst of all is when we are lost in grief or despair and you meet us with silence, absence.

It is so hard then to attend to you, God. We have been slow to learn the ways of being calm in the midst of uncertainty, of holding ourselves both empty and expectant for long stretches of time, of letting go of our need to be right or strong or well approved. When you seek to teach us these lessons through the events of our lives, deal tenderly with us, God, for we are afraid. Be patient with our weakness, merciful toward our failures, gentle with our ignorance. Forgive our inability to say an unreserved, unqualified "Yes" to you.

But take our partial "Yes's." Take our dim understandings. Take our hesitant faith. Take our half-love. Fan them with the breath of your Spirit that they may lead us more wholeheartedly into submission to your will. Tear like the wind through our clouds of doubt and pessimism. If life must be hard, O God, then may it be hard in your service rather than in futility. If we cannot escape suffering, then may our suffering be to your purposes. Remind us each morning that we may choose anew to move toward life or death, toward wholeness or fragmentation, toward love or meaninglessness. Give us the wisdom and courage we need each day, each hour. Amen.

Palm Sunday I

Spirit of love and power, you humbly steal into our lives, catching us unawares, so that we find ourselves laughing, dancing, singing, shouting. May we remember our glad hosannas of today when harsher realities tempt us to doubt your goodness. May we remember your irresistible tenderness when the world tempts us to idolize the forces of death. We would be one with the throng that follows your beloved Jesus into a new age. So shall we work with joy and lie down in peace, knowing the end is in your keeping. Amen.

Palm Sunday II

Strange, God, are the ways you conquer. With weakness rather than power, with humility rather than majesty, you crumble our defenses. You know our fear yet choose to trust in the courage you have planted in us. You see our self-absorption but have faith in our yearning to love. You know the evil we can do and still you believe in the goodness you breathed into us at our birth. How could you make yourself so vulnerable to us? How can we turn away from your suffering? How can we resist you? God, we must name you victor. Amen.

Maundy Thursday

Dear God, strange are the ways you draw us to yourself. In lowliness you kneel before us in the person of Jesus. Tenderly you wash us. In quiet love you serve us. You ask nothing for yourself but that we love each other. Thank you for turning power and glory inside out, so that to see you again we need only break honest bread and share a cup of kindness. Give us hearts, O God, simple enough to take you at your word. Amen.

· EASTER ·

Signs of Life

Living God, astound us once more with signs of your presence. In the withered corners of our love, amaze us with small, swelling buds. In the dead center of our despair, astonish us with tender shoots of hope. Across the barren fields of betrayal, let our bewildered eyes open to the greening of forgiveness. Into the frozen certainties of our endings, breathe warmth, that faith again may flower and exude the honey-damp fragrance of life. All praise and thanks to you, surprising God. Amen.

Roll Away the Stone

God, we have such a hard time "getting it." Every year we listen again to the story of Easter and still we look around us, puzzled. We are still concerned: who will roll away the stone at the entrance to the tomb?

We see that there continue to be wars and refugees from wars; outlaws and totalitarian regimes; cruelty and oppression; violence, accidents, and sickness. Who will roll away this stone of death?

We are horrified at the ways poverty and indifference set up ever-expanding slums. We hear people cry out, with rage on their tongues and hurt in their eyes. Who will roll away the stone of injustice?

We listen to voices, insistent and arrogant, that urge us to take matters into our own hands and protect ourselves. But that does not ease our terror of the stone, which weighs ever more heavily on our minds.

God, we are not even clear what side of this stone we stand on. We feel its mass of pain and fear and bitterness pressing against our hearts. We feel helpless, victimized, not quite good enough and very much alone. Are we in the clutches of death within the cold, dark confines of a rocky vault? Or are we dazedly walking in an outer world made meaningless because love and wisdom and life itself lie buried? We perceive only that there is a huge stone between the world we now inhabit and your heavenly commonwealth, O God. Who will roll away this stone? God, help us; help all your suffering earth, we pray.

So we come this morning. We come with our questions and our hope, with despair over the faults within us and the evil around us, with deep yearning for joy and goodness and life. We come not knowing who will roll the stone away, or how, but we come, finally, because your Spirit, God, compels us to come. We come to Easter and discover the stone is rolled away. Oh, it is still there, its weight of suffering as enormous as ever, but pushed aside, no longer able to separate us from you.

We thought, somehow, that it was all going to be left up to us, and here the stone has been moved by nothing we said or did or prayed, but only through the gracious power of your love, God. This we did not expect. This we find hard to even imagine. This is not our ordinary reality. It is wonderful, awful, joyous, terrifying. We stand, shocked, on the threshold which the stone once blocked. Do we dare cross? Do we run? Do we stay or go? Press forward or retreat? What is in the unknown beyond?

And then comes your voice, familiar, tender, calling us by name, and although everything looks the same, nothing will ever be the same again. We are aware of ourselves, no longer ourselves but more ourselves than ever. We are dissolved, centered, transported, grounded, empty, fulfilled. Nothing matters. Everything matters. And all is simply one, long, glorious Alleluia. Amen.

A New Line of Work
(JOHN 21)

God, it is often so hard for us to change our ways of doing things, our ways of looking at life. We have spent so much time learning how to fish and then you come and ask us to feed sheep.

We are disconcerted, surprised, confused. How we wish you would let us be, to fish in peace, whether we catch anything or not! After all our struggling to be content with—or at least accepting of—the status quo, you come and shake everything up. You find ways to tell us—laughingly or angrily, gently or daringly—that *you* are not content with how things are, that you have something better in mind for us and for our world. Deepen our understanding of where in our lives you are yearning for us to love you more. Amen.

Living Water

God of all our being, our souls thirst for life as deer pant for flowing streams. We sample many wells in our search for living water, knowing we want you but little knowing how to find you. Help us to persevere in our search for your presence in our lives. Grant us the faith to wait patiently on your timing, to trust that everything needful will be provided.

In times of loss or loneliness, bear us gently on the current of your love. When we feel overstressed or anxious, may we find respite in some quiet, shaded pool where we can gather strength and courage to go on. If we feel trapped in an eddy going nowhere, lift our vision to the passing shore. May we discover a peacefulness unknown to those swept up in swifter currents. When we are afraid of what the future may bring, God, give us that steady concentration on the present moment that allows us to navigate through dangers safely, perhaps even with exhilaration, as we discover again that you are continually sustaining us, enabling us both to will and to work for your good pleasure.

God, we give you thanks today for the joys of water:
  for its changeable beauty that dazzles or calms or awes us,
  for all the possibilities of play it offers, in both summer and
    winter,
  for its ability to wash things clean,
  for the refreshment it gives our bodies—cooling the throat
    and soothing the skin.

Remind us how precious water is, how necessary for all life on earth. Forgive our wastefulness and our mindless pollution. Forgive the arrogance with which we attempt to claim and control all water for our own purposes.

We pray for all people who have little or no clean water:
for those who must walk many miles every day to obtain
water,
for those who have no fuel to boil and purify tainted water,
for those whose water supply has been disrupted by war,
for those whose wells have been poisoned by the waste of
others too ignorant, careless, or greedy to note the harm done.

Show us, God, how we may best give a cup of cold water in
your name.

We pray for people who have traditionally relied on lakes
and seas for their livelihood, whose living has always been sub-
ject to the danger of storms, but who now also find access to
many fishing grounds impeded, fishing stocks depleted, and
what remains contaminated. We pray for all creatures who have
suffered because of human abuse of rivers, lakes, and oceans.
Show us, God, how we may best let justice roll down like water.

We await the outpouring of your Spirit, raining grace on the
just and the unjust, flooding a parched and thirsty world with
mercy, drowning the voices of those who prey on the fears and
desperations of your people. Holy Spirit, come! Amen.

Spirit Moves
O, God, we praise you for all things that move—
The random leaps and tumbles of fire and storm clouds,
Air that vibrates with music and laughter,
Rhythmic ocean swells that roll and break and recede and
roll,
Fluttering aspen leaves,
The spiraling hawk,
The beating heart,
All furry, four-footed young at play,
The earth itself whose stately spin draws sun and stars across
the sky, whose steady course carries us through the sea-
sons.

We praise you for the movement of our own lives—
   The learning, growing, letting go, and rebirth,
   The turns of mind, the softening of heart,
   Our voyages out and our journeys home.

Above all, we praise you for the movement of your Spirit, continually infusing
   all creation with your loveliness,
   all time with your holiness,
   all life with your image.

Like breath, like wind, your Spirit moves and we know its power by the fresh hope and new life that spring up at its passing. May all who suffer from grief or pain feel again its healing, quickening surge.

Send this Holy Spirit, we pray, into the world's shadowy corners to shred the clouds of hatred, greed, and fear that oppress whole countries; that dim many a city street; that hang over the lives of abused children and battered spouses.

Fan the flames of compassion to lighten the shadowy corners of our own hearts, O God. Help us to renounce our self-centered ways, and learn afresh how much our well-being depends on the well-being of others. May we greet misfortune with courage and hail good fortune with humility and generosity, knowing that we are forever held in your love. Amen.

Weight of Awe

God of mystery and majesty, can we draw close to you except in awe? Yet awe presses heavily upon our spirits. We feel unable to long sustain the weight of unknowing, the ache of fearful joy, the anxiety of losing ourselves in the strange otherworld of awe.

We say, let prophets and priests and saints be our intermediaries; let them dare your fiery presence and interpret your will to us. We are quite sure we will be content with ordinary health and prosperity. No need to encounter holiness. You don't call everyone to such dizzying heights, do you?

Why, then, do we experience these occasional stirrings of unrest? Why the feeling of hollowness within the complex fullness of our days? Why can we not stop asking, What does it mean? Really, God, all we want is a little peace.

But you laugh at our little peace. You blow into our lives uninvited, scattering signs and visions. Scary thoughts and powerful ideas swirl in your wake. Desperately, we try clinging to traditions that once proved reliable. To no avail. They are shredded in your wind. We can no longer pretend to be in control.

We can no longer avoid wondering whether even *you* are in control. Death stalks the streets. From here to Liberia your people are being killed. From here to Myanmar truth is twisted, mocked, and trampled upon. The land is seeded with mines, the air is full of holes, diseases wait in ambush. We are living in the last days. Truly, people always have been living in the last days, and your dread presence is all that has ever stood between us and destruction.

And so, as always in last days, you speak to each of us, in each one's own language, saying, "I am your God."

"I am your God," sounds for everyone through the green burning trees.

"You are standing on holy ground," exults the moist or dusty earth everywhere.

"You, you sitting in the sunlight, firelight, TV-light, or traffic light, you are my people."

And neither bird call nor thunder crash, neither telephone ring nor jet roar obscures the insistent demand, the persistent promise, "My people shall be a holy people."

Holy God, in these ordinary, windblown, last days, preserve us. Too much awareness and a baby's smile, a petal's fall, a piece of broken bread, a trembling cup will shatter us. We cannot alone bear such great awe; we cannot alone bear your love. Amen.

Timing

God, sometimes we want nothing more than to be able to stop and relax, but the winds of your Spirit push us into the wild future. Sometimes we would be glad to leave a place grown dull and heavy, but the weight of your Spirit says, "Stay." Grant us, God, a better sense of your timing, so that while it is day we may work with energy and joy, and when it is night we may peacefully rest. Whether we are busy or still, may we hold confidently to your promise that in everything you are at work for good for those who love you. So may your goodness bear fruit in us. Amen.

Tangles

O God, with astonishment we consider your works. The world is so tangled in beauty and rage, love and fear. What does this mean? We feel now buffeted, now caressed by the winds of your Spirit. Well, then, blow us together into the corner of your embrace. Break us, mend us, move us, change us, until our gathered joy spirals up in laughter and our shared grief crumbles into dust. Amen.

SACRAMENTS AND OTHER CELEBRATIONS

· BAPTISM ·

Practice Makes Perfect

Thank you, God, for signs that point to spring beyond winter, for faith that allows us to let go in order to receive, for rituals through which we practice dying and being reborn. Keep our eyes open to your Spirit at work in us. Keep our hearts tender toward your world around us. Keep our minds fixed on the joy before us as, day by day, you conform us more fully to Christ. Amen.

Through the Water

God, you ask such a lot of us. You seem to expect us to step forward, right into the water, straight down into the sea of our fears.

Surely you know this is too much for us. We stand, paralyzed, backs turned, unable to look upon the waves of shame, loss, grief, pain, death lapping at our heels. We can feel the panic threatening to engulf us. There must be another way! Where now is Moses with his mighty rod? Where is Miriam with her songs of victory?

Perhaps we were foolish to come here today. We thought to find celebration or comfort or stirring inspiration. We intended to sing your praises, to pray for other, oppressed people, to give you thanks for many blessings and then to return home. It didn't occur to us that you could have different plans. It never really dawned on us that we might not be able to go back. We forgot that our true home might wait for us in a land on the far side of breath.

What does it mean, God, that you follow behind us, a towering mystery of cloud? Do you guard us from some pursuing evil that would enslave us? Do you urge us on toward the vast waters of an unknown and terrifying glory? Did we pray for such a deliverance, God? Did we ever implore you for this dramatic a release from our troubles? Did *we* seek a covenant that would demand this kind of faith? If so, we didn't know what we were asking.

Ah, God, you have been here before, haven't you? If you are still willing to make of us a people for yourself, then send your breeze, a steady wind, across these floods again. Divide the waters of dread, walls of anxious doubt to one side and cold chaos to the other. We are not the first to pass down this way, nor are we alone; how great a crowd of your faithful ones goes with us! They, too, have been afraid; they, too, may have looked back with tears and longing for what is no more.

Bring us through together, God; bring us through death into a joyous, whole, new life in Christ together. Amen.

Water of Life

Thank you, God, for the wonder of water. Essential to life, as holy to protozoan as to redwood, as sacred to minnow as to human, water proclaims your mystery and your grace. In the awe of ocean expanse, in the joy of rushing streams, in the grief of human tears, in the peace of gentle rain, water sings of life. So we take water as a sign of your great love for us and bind ourselves together as your people with its mark. Amen.

· COMMUNION ·

Eucharist

God, source and sustainer of life, thank you for food. Thank you for the plants and animals that nourish our bodies. Thank you for the pleasures of crispy, crunchy, creamy, chewy textures, the delights of bitter, sweet, spicy, sour, salty, meaty, leafy flavor. Help us to honor the life that feeds us, the labor that brings food to our tables. Thank you for the privilege of being able to share our abundance. Direct our words, guide our actions to enable more people to experience the simple joy of giving food to others.

Thank you, God, for ideas and artistry that nourish our minds. Thank you for the wonder of words, music, color, line, symbol, and number. Thank you for the pleasures of learning, teaching, creativity, discovery, connection. Let our vision be clear, our dreams noble, and our communications truthful. Bring healing to those whose minds betray them, whose memories torture them, whose mental illnesses distort reality. Help the people around them to silence condemnation, control irritation, and refrain from condescension. Open our eyes to the gifts they bring and fill all our minds with the knowledge of your love and power and peace.

Thank you, God, for the kindness and respect that nourish our hearts. Thank you for expressions of caring, gratitude, appreciation, and love; for letters, cards, gifts, pats on the back, eyes glowing with pride or wet with tenderness. Thank you for feast days, parties, celebrations, gatherings that affirm the bonds among us. Thank you for the forgiveness that teaches us how to forgive, the trustworthiness that teaches us how to trust. We give you thanks for friends who understand us and enjoy our idiosyncrasies, friends who offer us both empathy and reminders of the best that is in us. Through our own deeds of compassion and generosity may our hearts keep growing stronger and wiser each day.

Thank you, God, for this day of communion, when we share food for body, mind, and heart. In ways beyond our understanding, deeper than our knowing, you come to us and offer us yourself. Can we partake together in your being and ever look at each other in the same way again? Can we eat love and go home unchanged? Thank you, God, for nourishing our spirits with your Spirit, through Jesus Christ. Amen.

Spirit Cup

From the cup of your Spirit, God, we drink healing. Bless to us this bittersweet flavor of loss and forgiveness, of pain and new life. You know how much we crave what is good and how fearful we are of its taste. Dissolve our lonely ambivalence in the pure resolve of Christ, so that together we may take strength for today and savor joy in each moment. Then may our lives brim over with the waters of peace to the glory of your name. Amen.

· STEWARDSHIP ·

Entrusted

God, you have entrusted us with the care of great beauty and enormous wealth. We feel in turns honored, careless, possessive, and helpless in the face of such providence. Do you mean we have to figure out together how to live with this abundance? We are so much better at dividing, hoarding, spending, and claiming little pieces. God, open our hearts and minds and hands that we may grow into the fruitful, generous images of yourself that you made us to be. Amen.

Mother's Day

Living God, thank you for the women who gave us life: for the women whose bodies were our first homes, providing food, comfort, warmth, and birth into new life; for the women who rocked us, sang to us, bathed us, carried us in weary arms, and tended to our middle-of-the-night alarms; who taught us, shielded us, and launched us toward selfhood; for the women who smiled on us with pride or encouragement or just for the delight of being with us.

Thank you for the women who have mothered us.

God, there are some of us here today who are missing our mothers: because of death, because of vast physical or emotional distance, because disease has made them strangers, because we do not know how to mend a relationship that is frayed, torn, in shreds. And some of us are missing children: children who were and are no more, longed-for children never born. Come to us, God, in the cold, outer reaches of grief and loneliness. Sew us new garments. Clothe us with hope, wrap us in a stronger vision, drape us with patience and faith in your promises for a future bright with purpose and warm with meaning.

Thank you for your tenderness toward all who are bereft.

God, there are some of us today who are disoriented by shifting patterns of motherhood. As step-parents or noncustodial parents, adoptive parents or single parents, we are especially apt to puzzle over how to nurture the children given into our care. As children we wonder how to love without "taking sides." How do we live, God, surrounded by broken dreams and unknown frontiers, premature endings and weighty new beginnings?

Embed us, we pray, in a community of wisdom and compassion. Let kindness and honesty, humility and mercy guide our words and actions. Thank you for walking with us across strange and unfamiliar territory. Thank you for the people who have gone before us and left markers along the way.

God, there are some of us today who feel abundantly blessed, for we are joined with others in the joyful dance of giving and receiving love. We have held others close and been held close. We have been lifted up and lifted others up. We have swung each other until, dizzy with laughter, we have fallen together in a happy heap. For the difficult maneuvers we have been given good tutors. We have known the comfort of following and the pleasure of improvising. We are able simply to dance well enough.

Thank you, God, for all life-giving connections. Thank you for making yourself known to us in and through them. Thank you for dancing with us as mother, as child, as our heart's delight. Amen.

Father's Day

God, today is a day we have set apart to remember men who are fathers. For those of us who have known the loving attention and guidance of a good father, it is easy to give thanks today.

Thank you for men for whom there is an uncomplicated joy in teaching, caring for, and playing with children.

Thank you for men who gladly assume the responsibilities that come with fathering a child and are willing to put their children's needs on a par with their own.

Thank you for men who allow their sons and daughters to teach them to become the parent they need.

Ease them through their worries, guide them in their hopes. May these fathers know your blessing through the lifelong love and respect of their children.

God, hold in tenderness men who long to father a child and still have not. If your time is not yet, grant them patient faith. And if they are never to become birth fathers, open them to the possibility that you are leading into their lives other children who need their care and will return their love. We know that today can be painful for men who have lost children to disease, accident, or violence. Sustain them in faith and bring them your peace.

God, bestow your wisdom and guidance on men who have never themselves known the love of a father. Help them if they struggle to comprehend what being a good father means. Stand close with those whose understanding of fatherhood does not match the traditional images society prescribes and yet whose children thrive in their care.

With compelling grace intervene, God, in the lives of men who have become fathers carelessly or unintentionally; in the lives of men who lack in material or spiritual resources to support their children; in the lives of men who feel powerless to be a positive presence in the lives of their sons and daughters or who feel powerful only when they are violent. Grant them courage and insight into the ways you would have them go.

We pray also for fathers who feel alienated from their children, who neither understand them nor feel understood by them. They may yearn simply for respect or a small but genuine sign of affection. We ask that you work your healing reconciliation in such families.

Most of all, we rejoice today in the large number of men who manage to be "good enough" fathers, God. "Good enough" that their children prosper and learn and grow up to ask your blessings on fatherhood. "Good enough" that we feel neither ashamed nor bitter nor afraid to call you "Father." "Good enough" that we can move beyond the limits and mistakes of our human love to begin to imagine the extent of your fatherly love for this world. Amen.

Labor Day I
God bless our labor. We labor for good things—for bread and fruit and a handful of flowers; for clothes and health and a warm,

soft bed. We labor to provide not only for ourselves, but for those we love: spouse, child, friend in need. Grant, therefore, that our labor enrich and not deplete our relationships.

Bless our labor, God, that it may bring blessings to others. If we serve, let it be with cheerfulness; if we teach, let it be with enthusiasm; if we sell, with honesty; if we buy, with astuteness; if we manage, with diligence; if we care for people, with kindness. Thank you for all the many other people who make it possible for us to do our work well, the family members and neighbors, friends and coworkers, mentors and employees whom we often take for granted, but for whom we are truly grateful.

Bless our labor, God, that it may be a source of spiritual growth. We know the value of work lies beyond measures of money or fame. We ask of you, therefore, some work that demands creativity and some work that builds patience, some work that enlarges our horizons and some work that remains within our limitations, some work that contributes to a noble end and some work that makes us nobler beings.

Forgive us when we grumble about our work, whether we complain about certain tasks or procedures or people. Help us to change what we need to change—our job, our environment, our attitude. May we discover within the absurdities of work the gift of laughter. Do not let us acquiesce, out of laziness or greed or fear, to work that destroys our integrity. Neither let us become so attached to our work that our whole sense of self becomes wrapped up in what we do. When we encounter the pain of losing a job, the pain of finding that we are not indispensable, the pain of discovering that no one seems to want our skills, keep us from despair. Do you not always have work for us, God—the work of expressing your loving presence?

Bless our labor, God, that it may be the true gift of true self, a service of heart and mind, hand and strength. May our work be joy and our joy your praise. Amen.

Labor Day II

All wise and compassionate God, thank you for creating each of us with the need and the capacity to work and to love. Thank you for the joy of self-abandonment in doing the work to which we are truly called and in sharing the love for which we are expressly fashioned. Grant us the courage and the persistence, we pray, to do the tasks you have equipped us to do, even when the world accords us little status or reward for such work. Help us to be wise and gentle with each other in the giving and receiving of care lest we become overly preoccupied with merely pleasing others or with only satisfying our own desires. By your grace, may we discover and rediscover the places where the world's deep longings and our own deep gladness meet. Thank you for the freedom we have in our land to work out our own salvation as your Spirit gives us guidance, to live in peace with our neighbor, and to pursue happiness for ourselves and our children.

There are times, O God, when we fear we are not made for happiness—times when it seems that everyone except us has it all together; times when the notion of meaningful work seems like a luxury we can't afford; times when we are steeped in loneliness and grief; times when pain gnaws at our bones. There are days that stretch into weeks and months—sometimes even years—when we despair of ever knowing deep gladness. Hold us close in those times, dear God. Come to us in the guise of a friend or stranger, a relative or professional who offers us understanding and the assurance that we are seen and known and cared for. Help us, also, to recognize ones to whom we may offer such understanding and assurance. So may our longings meet the full, deep gladness of Christ. Amen.

SEASONAL PRAYERS

∞

· WINTER ·

Holy Time

Thank you, God, for the gift of this day you have made. We would rejoice and be glad in its charms, carrying us moment by moment to new life. Yet often we feel so caught up in the whirl of time, it seems more like a race with death. We long for life at a human pace, a breathing pace, a heart pace. Is there some demon on our backs, whispering in our ears, faster, faster, better, more; seize the day, improve each shining moment, time and tide wait for no one? Free us, O God, from this trickster who promises power, glory, security, control—but takes our souls as payment.

Free us to slow down enough to see, to wonder, to follow after random beauty.

Free us to hear, to learn, to pay attention to the mystery in the world, in our neighbors, in ourselves.

Free us to be trusting and empty, humble and merry.

God, if we sometimes squander time to avoid an unpleasant, but needful task, redirect our steps and arm us with courage. If we sometimes fool ourselves about the importance of a petty chore, lure us onto a wiser path. You know how hard it is for us, on the best of days, to weigh all the claims on our hours—so many for the job, so many for family; these for me, those for friends; a few moments for the community, a few for you. If it keeps adding up to more than a day's worth, what are we to give up?

God, teach us the secret of making time our servant rather than our master. Teach us how to dance with the minutes that twist into the thread of life. We will know then that it can be a sacred use of time to wait, watching for the treetops to catch the morning light; to enjoy the feathered tracery of frost across a window; to hear the whistle of a cardinal and the low rumble of the furnace; to smell soup or coffee or bread. Time spent reading poetry, eating snowflakes, walking with a friend, or praying will then truly be time blessed.

Help us, God, to move with grace among scheduled and unscheduled moments. Help us to trust that you always provide the time that is needful: time for grief to honor the dead, time for caresses to honor the living; time to meet eyes, to connect lives, to go the long way around, to laugh; time to compost peevish words, to bury grudges, to sprout healing, to grow forgiveness.

Gratefully, we acknowledge that this day is holy because you have entered into it with us, God. Therefore, we will rejoice and be glad. Amen.

January Praises

God among us, God within us, God beyond us, all we know of you calls out for our praise.

We praise you for beauty the earth breathes forth at your command and for beauty distilled, crafted, sung by human minds, hands, and voices. Beauty itself declares your praise.

We praise you for January days, white and blue-shadowed, vaporous, crackling stiffly as cold fire. We praise you, for we have warm buildings, soft beds, hot coffee, and windows between us and the snow and sunlight. O God, look tenderly on all who have no shield between them and winter. Open our eyes to those whose needs you have equipped us to meet. May we know only restlessness until we are moving in concert with your will.

We praise you, God, for those particular people, ideas, and activities that you have given into our care. The passion we bring to love and work proclaims your praise.

We praise you for memories, hard-soft as mothers' hands, plain as grass, fanciful as flight, nestled in our hearts. We praise you, for we have snapshots of happy-eyed childhood, richly embroidered stories, persons to hold our hands. O God, gently embrace all who have no guard between them and horror. Open our arms to those whose pain we have the power to allay. May we know peace only as we contribute to the peace of those around us.

We praise you, God, for children, dawn creatures, unformed, hungry, insistent, trusting us for wisdom to a degree that is frightening. Take our love and good intentions; let them be enough to counter our ignorance and failings. Help us to nourish well their bodies, hearts, minds, and spirits that they may live fully, as you intend. May their joy in life infect our hearts. Children's laughter shouts your praise.

We praise you for hope, rugged and mountain high, horizon-tinged, and rooted deeply as an oak. We praise you, for we have been given strong-valued foundations, long-visioned heroes, fourth and fifth chances, resources to make choices. Compassionate God, hold close all who have no shelter from despair. Open our hearts to those whose fears would be eased by the gift of our presence. May we view injustices with neither resignation nor a sense of futility, but with faith in your power to work through us to bring good. We seldom know what small deed of ours may inspire another to dream and plan and work for justice. This, too, is a marvelous work of yours.

Therefore, praise, all praise, we offer to you, great God. Let songs of your goodness never cease; let psalms of your faithfulness be sung forever. Amen.

Midwinter Souls

God of our longing, you are as silent as sunlight, as invisible as warmth. Rise on us like dawn, dissipating our frosty fears and dispelling the gloom of our narrow minds. Slowly, tenderly warm our frostbitten spirits. As much as we crave new life, the returning flow of circulation hurts. The cold often feels like a friend, locking up the pain we'd rather not feel. Give us courage to grieve for all that may be lost to us: the voice of a loved one, youthful vitality, meaningful work, a known identity, security, or even our dreams. May your consoling peace seep deeply into our bones.

Merciful God, grant us fortitude to endure all that we must simply live through and guidance to change all that causes needless suffering. Melt our frozen hearts, that we may be less quick to criticize the motives and activities of our partners, our children, our colleagues, our neighbors. Free us from the cold comfort of our individual certainties. Brush the snow out of our eyes so that we can see the hurts and anxieties of those with whom we disagree. Kindle graciousness and compassion in our souls.

God, how we yearn for spring when beyond our own doors so much of the world seems to be in the grip of wintry hatred and icy fear. What floods of joy could be released were it all to melt away in the sunshine of your righteous love! And how afraid we are of the chaos that floods always bring. So it is with some hesitancy and a little doubt, with much hope and a growing faith, that we pray to you, O fiery God. Bring your people together to act as lenses, focusing your light on oppression and violence. May the old, crusty, dirty white mantle of prejudice and privilege that blankets our world thaw. Give us promising glimpses of the dark soil, the softening earth, the waiting seedbed, beneath.

Attune us to your seasons, God, that we may work patiently, faithfully, and with integrity at the tasks nearest us, trusting you to bring forth the green shoot and the tender blossom when your time has come. Amen.

Spare Beauty

Thank you, God, for spare beauty: for the bare branch, the black furrow, skim ice, and bird flight. Thank you for the stripping away that reveals far horizons. Thank you for distance that conjures wider mystery. You have given us the joy of knowledge and the pleasure of wonder. All praise to you, plain and hidden God. Amen.

∞

· SPRING ·

Breath of Spring

Thank you, God, for the breath of spring, sweet with sunlight, damp with lilacs, heavy with memory. Green washes over us, as fresh as tomorrow, as old as the hills. We swing between nostalgia and hope. It is good to remember, God, who we are and from where we come. And it is good to look forward, to give to the future as freely and generously as we receive from the past. Thank you, God, for holding us, past, present, and future, within the bright, eternal flow of your Spirit. Amen.

Growing

God, sometimes we are reluctant to lose the sheaths that protect us. We marvel at the ease with which trees release their bud-protecting scales, exposing tender petals and new leaves to wind and frost and rain. It is dangerous to grow, God—dangerous, exhilarating, and lovely. Tease us with your ardent warmth until we drop the precautions that confine us. Call up in us a surge of strong sweet sap until we have no choice but to break forth in a beauty to make all hearts sing. Urge us deep and wide and high until we reach together our full stature in Christ. Amen.

Nesting God

God, in our cupped and waiting hearts, come build your nest. Wedge your Spirit firmly into the angles of our lives. Make here a home to shelter the frail, the poor, the little ones. Weave in kindness, line it with laughter, cover it over with your faithfulness. We will stand tender guard, attentive, rooted, and still, listening for your clear, sweet song as you rejoice over your creation. Come, O God, rest in the branches of our hearts. Amen.

Revelations of April

God, life is so much like April: one moment bright and golden warm; another sodden, gray, and cold. Yet buds keep swelling, birds continue to sing their return, green creeps across the earth and through the trees. Help us to recognize our own soul's persistence in growth, sometimes hidden deep within us, sometimes surging across the landscape of our lives in explosions of color. With the unfolding of each day, may we come to trust more fully in your process, in life's goodness, and in our capacity to love. Thank you, God, for the slow, sweet revelations of spring. Amen.

Spirit Flow

Spirit of holiness, sink deep within us. Enter the very sap of our being. Course through the cracks of our fears and griefs, coaxing us to growth and healing. Flow into our hungry roots, to anchor us during whatever storms will rage. May your sweetness both renew our lives and bring joy to the garden in which we are planted. Holy Spirit, Spirit of Life, all praise and thanks to you. Amen.

Starter of Seeds

Thank you, God, for planting your Spirit within us. We have tried to guard and cherish this windblown seed as it sprouts and grows. By what chemistry does faith bud and swell and bloom? Such a bright sweet flower must have had its beginnings in a heavenly field. We are in awe that neither flood nor drought nor storm can flatten its loveliness. Now may the beauty of blossom ripen into the round goodness of fruit so that all may taste your bounty and give glory to you. Amen.

Thirst for Life

God of all our hopes, to you we bring our longings for wholeness and peace. When there is such mass suffering in the world, our individual pains may seem trivial, yet they can destroy us as they gnaw away at our souls. The death of someone close to us, our own ill health or that of someone we love, conflict with a family member or work colleague, financial worries, the loss of meaning in our life—any of these may cause us to close in upon ourselves and to fear that the cup of despair has no bottom. Have mercy on us, O God.

Deep, deep into your love, we send our roots, thirsting for life. Let your healing rise up in us so that what was dry and withered becomes soft and full and green; unfolding shiny, never-before-seen moments. With warmth and sun and misty rain, coax us to stretch, to open, to make room again for laughter.

As you patiently restore us to life, O God, gently prune away the tangles of anxiety, the sprouts of bitterness, the dead wood of past wrongs. Cut and shape and reveal the beauty in each one of us. Allow us each to bless the world with color or fragrance or shelter or fruit. Let us delight in the gifts we bring to each other. Hear the singing of our hearts, as we rejoice in your power to bring life from death, to open out possibilities from once dead ends. Amen.

In the Garden

God, we come together on this summer day, glad for the sun and the green and the gentle breeze scented with flowers. Thank you for the power of beauty to lift our spirits. Take our dawn-dizzy minds and earthy hands, take our sun-dazed souls and fertile hearts to build your garden, God. Clip and prune and stake us as you will; cultivate, water, and mulch, until we breathe forth the scent of kindness, the odor of wisdom, and the smell of holiness. Amen.

Signs of God's Presence

God, wherever we find loveliness, goodness, or peace, we see the imprint of your hand. And seeing signs of your presence, we rejoice and give thanks.

Thank you for all the beauty of high summer: for dark woods, fragrant, damp, and cool; for bright countrysides where wind plays in tall roadside grasses and across the ripening fields; for richly colored gardens yielding delights to eye and nose and tongue. Thank you for all wayward charms: a flash of oriole orange among the treetops; the intricate dance of a pair of swallowtails; a jumping fish momentarily breaking a soft evening silence; overheard notes of a child singing to herself. At such times we know this earth is a wonderful place to call home and we offer our gratitude to you for the abundance of its gifts.

Thank you, God, for the goodness of people: for all eagerness to provide for others time, care, things useful and beautiful; for all generosity of spirit that loudly applauds accomplishment and quietly forgives mistakes; for all graciousness in the giving and receiving of hospitality; for all courage and perseverance in seeking a greater wisdom, pursuing a truer justice, and developing a deeper peace for the world.

Thank you for those who, by their very being, make life more enjoyable for others. Whether by their smiles, their humorous outlook on life, their openness to others' happiness and pain, the lilt in their voices, or the skip in their walk, some people just make us glad we share the earth with them. With deep gratitude, we remember before you the many individuals who have blessed our lives. Help us, likewise, to be blessings to others. Amen.

Wealth of June

Dear God, how you weigh us down with the wealth of June: gold sunlight, silver rain, the jewels of countless flowers. You pile on scent and thunderous sound. And what of the load of spiritual riches under which we stagger? Great mountains of awe, vast oceans of love press down on us. It is too much for our hearts to hold, too huge for our minds to comprehend. It is all we can do to breathe. Ah, wondrous God! Amen.

Abundance

Thank you, God, for sensuous riches—
  For the color in sumac and apple, pumpkin and sunflower,
    aspen and sky.
  For the pleasure of sound in surf and wind, frog and
    meadowlark, trumpet, organ, and harp.
  For the weight of scent in wood smoke and damp leaves,
    cinnamon and lavender, hay and sweet fern and baby hair.
  For the delights of touching feathers and moss, water and
    polished stone, beach sand, puppy ears, and fingertips.
Every movement, every breath reveals another facet of the
beauty with which you surround us.

Thank you, God, for the vast array of material things in our
universe—
  The uncountable billions of stars and beetles, the millions
    upon millions of salmon and snails, the ten thousand kinds
    of orchids and the thousands of species of birds.
  Thank you for salt and silver; opals and oil; granite and
    grasses; melons, magnolias, and morels.
  Thank you for cows and cats and llamas; walruses, turtles,
    bears, dolphins, gorillas, dogs, and kangaroos.

From lava to lightning, water lilies to pussy willows, hermit
crabs to human beings, you pile up wonder upon wonder and
whimsy upon whimsy.

Thank you, God, for all the intricate systems by which you sus-
tain life—
  For the physics of light and the perfection of water.
  For the alchemy wrought by chlorophyll and the dance of
    hemoglobin with oxygen.
  For chromosomes, membranes, root hairs, and nerves.

For all the humble beings of the earth—microbes and fungi
and worms—which turn death into new life.
We are awestruck at how precisely everything fits together.

Thank you, God, for the wealth of human connections, for the
treasury of talents you bestow for the well-being of all—
For vision and wisdom, compassion and judgment, dexterity,
artistry, industry, and husbandry.
For the abilities to comfort, teach, heal, and inspire.
For the qualities of patience, empathy, cheerfulness, serenity, and enthusiasm.

The magnitude of your providence, God, is overwhelming.
In sheer joy and naked gratitude we lay our lives before you.
Thank you, God; thank you, God. With all our heart and soul,
mind and strength, we breathe, Ah, God, thank you. Amen.

Beginnings

Holy God, we are gathered here in gratitude that you go before us in all our beginnings, accompany us in all our travels,
and bless us in all our endings.

As we cross the threshold of a new season, a new school year,
a new world order, we thank you for the feelings of anticipation, hope, excitement, and promise. Thank you for all that is
fresh, unspotted, and shiny, as full of possibilities as the newborn child or the dawning day.

Ever-creating One, you know only too well, however, that
we rarely face beginnings with unalloyed gladness. We do not
always welcome the unfamiliar and alien. Often we are anxious
or downright fearful. Help us, God. If you yourself are both deepest mystery and eternal presence, help us to trust that at the
center of every unknown city and wilderness, in the midst of
every new situation and event, in the soul of every stranger,
pulse your goodness and love.

Often, God, we do not recognize the necessity of endings before the arrival of beginnings. We stand before the closed door

of what once was, blinded by tears. Turn us in a new direction. Show us how to let go, embrace change, brave insecurity, live with loss. So many things we fear to lose and yet sometimes must lose: relationships, health, job, home, possessions, reputation, sanity, life itself. Sometimes, dear God, what we most need to lose is what we cling to most tightly—our hurt, anger, bitterness, arrogance, self-righteousness. How can we drop these shields and expose our frail selves to the world's cruelty? And some losses occur so subtly we are caught unawares by our pangs of grief. What can we do when we suddenly realize the absence of trust or hope or integrity or innocence or meaning? What can we do when we feel we have lost you?

O God, whose loving-kindness has neither beginning nor end, have mercy on us. Speak to us the word we need to hear. Tell us that while we may have lost all and even you, you do not lose us. Speak to us of light and new beginnings. Speak to us of dawn. Speak to us of resurrection. Amen.

Equinox

Holy and gracious God, let September live in us today. Make us vigorous as rain, gentle as the lowering light. Round our words into sweet fruit and stretch our hearts as wide as wheat fields. Steady us on strong, unhurried wings obedient to the beauty of your moment. Hold us serenely balanced between light and dark, work and rest, giving and gathering, keeping and letting go. May the fullness of this between-time be good and peaceful enough. Amen.

Not Ready

O God, all around us now the leaves are falling, blanketing streets and yards and parks with a patchwork of gold and brown. The falling leaves turn us into wild-eyed poets, lamenting the end of summer's warmth and bounty, railing against the encroaching darkness and cold. Another autumn finds us no more ready for winter than we were a year ago.

And if our yards and homes and cars and minds are not yet quite ready to grapple with the changing season, still less are our spirits. Rare, indeed, is the moment when we can say to you, "Yes, God, it is time for me to enter the icy valley of the shadow of death with you." The paths of loss and grief and pain are not ones we take willingly even when we are convinced they lead to growth and new life—let alone when we are overwhelmed by doubts that spring will ever again come for us.

Help us, God, in our weakness and limited vision. Knit us together in a community that shoulders one another's burdens and offers sustenance in times of need. By your grace may we gain the courage to cease our denials. Help us, God, to prepare together for life beyond death.

And then in faith we will bury seemingly lifeless bulbs deep into the earth. In faith we will wait.

In faith we will plant seemingly lifeless murmurs of peace and assurance in one another's ears. In faith we will hope.

In faith we will envision a future of golden flowers and radiant children. In faith we will labor and pray and encourage each other during fierce blizzards and long nights and cold grayness.

We will do this, God, trusting in your will and power to bring new life and joy to the world. Even in the knowledge of our own fear we look, trembling, to you, God, daring to say that we speak peace and plant love in the name of our crucified and risen Christ. Amen.

Ripening

Ripen us, God, as sun ripens corn and grapes. Round out the complex flavors of our lives. In the way that light departs from summer skies, sinking into grain and fruit, so let your Spirit weight us with rich thanksgiving and sweet compassion. Reap laughter, harvest song, and gather in all tears. Blend here our strengths and weaknesses to make for yourself a full-bodied praise. Glory, abundant glory, to you, O God. Amen.

∞

PRAYING FOR CHILDREN

∞

Eyes of the Unknown

Who are we, God, that you bother us with the eyes of children we don't know? What do you expect us to do about their rage, their hunger, their sadness, their infinitely dead resignation? We have neither love enough nor power enough to bring them to life and joy. We are weary of compassion, overwhelmed by the size of their need, and afraid of where you might ask us to go. Still, you do not allow us to turn away. Be with us, among us, gracious Spirit; for surely you alone have love enough and power enough to bring us all to life and to infuse us with the joy of serving one another. Amen.

Grateful and Anxious

Loving and faithful God, we come to you feeling both grateful and anxious for the world's children.

We are grateful for smiles and trusting eyes, for dimpled hands and cartwheeling limbs, for quick, quirky, questioning minds, for tender hearts and brave spirits. Thank you for surprising, amusing, and deeply touching young views of reality. Thank you for purple-popsicle tongues and grass-green knees, for muddy summer toes and snowflaked winter cheeks. How familiar and strange, how remarkable and ordinary these growing-up beings are. Our lives would be barren without them. Hear us, O God, as our hearts gratefully name the children who shake us with laughter and tears, hope and vitality.

God, a hard-edged world looms before our eyes and we fear for these children. We know too well the fragility of skin and brain and bone. We ponder the effects of pollution and violence on minds and emotions. Yet we can protect our children from only so much before imprisoning their spirits and distorting their vision. A cacophony of voices tells us Do! Don't! Should! Must not! But you, God, are trustworthy. Help us to find the wisdom you have planted within us all, young and old alike. Help our fearful love to unfold, open out, soar, dive deep, say joy, dance yes. Amen.

Gifts of Childhood

God, we long to be the kind of people that children can admire and trust. Visit us with your wisdom and your peace by which we may begin anew with fresh courage and resolve. We will remember the children we once were—how we giggled at the world's foolishness, wept over our losses, raged at all injustice, and yearned for acceptance. We will remember how you once came to us as a child, needy and vulnerable. We will remember earth's children and what glory you reveal to us through them. By your grace, may we have the privilege of feeding, clothing, soothing, shielding, healing, encouraging, guiding, or delighting in a child today. Then shall the taste of your goodness banish all anxiety from our hearts. Praise, all praise to you, O God, for the gifts of children. Amen.

Big Thanks for Small Beings

Thank you, God, for children:
for wide eyes and lashes damply closed on sleepy cheeks,
for shy smiles and impulsive kisses,
for minds and hands and legs in motion,
for their unquestioning trust in us.

Thank you, God, that children need us, because it is too easy
to forget how much we need them.
Thank you for their insistence on food and hugs; in
nourishing them we feed our own souls.
Thank you for their whines that teach us patience, for their
curiosity that primes our creativity,
for their demands for attention that keep us focused on life
here and now.
Thank you for their tears that remind us that it is necessary
and proper to grieve loss and pain.
Thank you for their surprising, unique selves.
Thank you, God, that children sleep.

We are grateful to children for keeping us close to little
things: ants and dandelions; feathers, rocks, and puddles.
They give us back the capacity to delight in the common,
to wonder at the ordinary, and so help us to recognize you,
God, in unexpected places. Amen.

Trust

Trusting ourselves to you is difficult, God, but it is even more
difficult to trust our children to you. In a small corner of our
minds we wonder whether you really do love them more than
we ever can or whether you really are powerful enough to keep
them safe. We want to protect our children from suffering—
even the same suffering that once taught us compassion. We
want to shield them from the painful mistakes that go with
learning to be responsible. We want to save them from random
hurts, careless wounds, and hard injustice that could either forge
their character or break them utterly. Help us to give them guidance without smothering them, to allow them freedom without neglecting them. Let there be many people in their lives
whom they love and who nurture their growth. So may they
learn with us the liberty of trusting you. Amen.

QUESTIONS

∞

Are You Sure?

Mysterious God, in the play between word and silence you bring worlds into being. You withdrew from nothing to make room for space. You spoke, and waves of matter tumbled onto shores of light. It is all too great and wonderful for us. Yet, you sit us down and say to us, "Look, see, create." You pull us to our feet and say, "Listen, hear, love." You turn us around and say, "Touch, feel, live." God, you are so much better at this creating, loving, and living than we are. So much pain accompanies our learning how. Are you sure this is what you had in mind?

Your silence draws the questions from us. We conceive answers upon answers, a tower reaching toward heaven, buttressed with metaphors on all sides, and discover we were closer to the truth when we accepted our confusion.

God, help us to become better at inquiry. Help us to build and love and live into the questions with more freedom and gaiety. When decisions must be made in the midst of doubt, help us choose in love and trust all outcomes to you. You know this is difficult for us. Is it difficult for you, too? Are you as frustrated by our distant coolness as we are by your silence?

God, you give us living warmth. We give you the sounds of heartbeat and breath. Make us one again, for we are lost without you. Amen.

Bent Things

Thank you, God, for things bent: for bird wing, warped tree, cat crouch, and conch shell; for runner's limbs, cellist's wrist, child's curled fingers. Thank you for things folded, pleated, tucked, and ridged; angled, jointed, and refracted; for the turn in the road, the bend in the river, the crook in the path; for question, doubt, and query.

Rather than prayers for perfect clarity, O God, help us to accept the limits to our sight as lures that draw us into glad wonder and mystery. Teach us to give ourselves over to the forces that shape and form and braid meaning into our lives. May we be bent as the arched bridge, the twisted rope, the bowed sail, the coiled spring—bent for strength and power, beauty and purpose. Knead the stiffness out of us, God, that we may flex rather than snap, may yield and adapt with grace to challenge. Make us lithe-minded and supple-hearted, the more readily to respond to your leading.

For as planets bend their travels to the sun, we would turn our lives to you, God. Weight us with your gravitational pull until we stoop to look closely into the faces of sad children and angry youths, fearful strangers and hurting people everywhere, and in stooping see your eyes looking back at us. Ah, God, it is hard thanks we give for this heavy recognition. Joined thus to suffering, we become agitated, angry, anxious. "Do something!" is our cry to you, to others, to ourselves. "Straighten this mess out!"

But what if, *what if* that were as foolish as straightening out a planet's path? What if your desire is to curve us, instead, into closer orbit? What if suffering—ours, theirs, yours—is simply to bend us all closer to you? God, what if? Bent and bending God, gently hold the deep and hidden places of our hurt and our resistance.

Thank you, God, for things bent and bowed and humble: the branch beneath the snow, long grass in the wind, brook around embedded stone. Neither in despair nor in resignation do we kneel before you, but in trust. May you find us more pliable each day, more willing to be conformed to Christ. Amen.

Changing the Rules

Holy Creator, thank you for the order you have made to regulate the movement of the universe. With the elegance of mathematics and the eloquence of philosophy, we try to understand your cosmos. If we pretend to know more than we do, look gently on our arrogance, O God. Do not let us forget the joy of gazing at the stars whose courses we chart, the pleasures of breathing in the air whose temperature we measure, the delight in tasting the fruit whose chemistry we determine. May the happiness we find through the mind's comprehension complement our sensual enjoyment of your creation.

Ordering and sustaining God, we are a people who like predictability. We are disconcerted when the rules seem suddenly to change. When we have attempted to build our lives around one set of values and voices begin calling those values into question, we feel angry and confused. When those voices are close to us—a partner, a friend, a son or daughter—we may feel betrayed. If I've spent so much effort teaching my child right from wrong, how can it be that she is arrested for shoplifting? If marriage is supposed to be lifelong, why is my spouse seeking a divorce? If I have always been there, through thick and thin, for my brother, why has he cut me out of his life? Why, God?

Help us, we pray, to live through the pain and anger of feeling betrayed.

Sometimes it is the whole culture that seems to have abruptly changed the rules. Which path do I take these days to be a good mother, a good father? How am I to behave as a woman, as a man? We once learned ways to be friendly to others that are now interpreted as evil or manipulative. We dedicated our lives to a career of service and are accused of being inept or power hungry. We have attempted to do the best we knew how and been told that it isn't good enough.

O God, help us to live through the pain and anger of confusion.

And sometimes, God, you seem to be the one who has changed the rules. When we live right and yet fall ill; when we try very hard to be loving and good and still suffer loss upon tragic loss; when we strive to love you, to do your will, yet you are hidden from us, what are we to think? Is all futility?

Help us, O God, to live through the pain and anger of feeling abandoned.

Bring us to new and deeper levels of truth. Show us how to trust in your underlying order, when to all appearances everything is chaos. Renew in us the determination to hold fast to virtue even when others break laws with impunity. Let neither fear nor suffering deter us from living responsibly and fully. So may it be, God, that we become acquainted with that peace that slowly grows in us when we are aligned with your purposes. Amen.

Choose Life

God, you give us the mounded hours of the day, each to be shaped by our choices. "Choose life," we hear you say, but it is not always clear what form "life" should take this moment. Are we to be engaged in serving others or in restoring our own energies? Is it a time to spend or a time to conserve? A time to listen or a time to make our voice heard? A time to sacrifice or a time to call others to account? How can we know?

Reason is a fallible guide when so many ghosts haunt the halls of our memories. Sound judgment gives way before the fears which stalk a deepening twilight. We are bedeviled by our insecurities, bewitched by sweet enticements. In the midst of shifting shadows it is hard to know what is real, what is solid, what is trustworthy, what is life-giving. We are not able to choose life, O God, without your guidance—not life for our planet, not life for our nation, not life for our families, not even life for ourselves. On some dull days we even forget what life means; we only know that we feel worried or bored or drained or dead.

"Choose life." Ah, if only we could, O God! Help us to understand!

You smile and take us gently by the hand. Perhaps you even chuckle a bit. And you tell us, "Your longing itself is a choice for life. You would escape your feelings of uncertainty or grief or pain, but they are as life-giving as the exhaling of breath or the death of worn-out cells. Listen to your fears, for they are the means by which you are connected to all other creatures. Honor your grief, for it enlarges your spirit, making more room for joy. Take your pain in both hands; turn it over and over; it will teach you humility, compassion, and maybe even wisdom.

"Do not be discouraged that it is so hard to choose life, because I am with you. I will neither abandon nor betray you. Often I will come to you in the guise of another, for the heart of life is relationship.

"Choose life."

God, we do this day choose life, praying only that you continue to remind us that all our choices are our gifts to you. Help us choose the true desires of our hearts. Amen.

Holes

Thank you, God, for holes: the hidden spring, the forest glade, the parting cloud, the river gorge, the leafy grotto. Thank you for holes that welcome in and send forth: gateways, doors, hearths, and chimneys; windows, hatches, chutes, and stairwells; ears and mouths and nostrils; ohs, ahs, hoorays, hosannas.

Thank you for caves, burrows, hollow trees, cleft rocks, bird nests, bee hives, harbors, and coves—for all holes that give shelter.

Thank you for holes of treasure: quarry, mine, and oil well; holes for music through flute and horn and organ pipe; holes of grace—loophole, Sabbath rest, storm's eye, a margin for error.

Yet some holes annoy us, God. There are limits to our gratitude. Holes worn in shoes or socks, moth-eaten sweaters; leaks in hoses, pipelines, tanks, boats, and roofs; broken fences, torn nets, potholes—what are they good for except extra work to mend, repair, or replace? Or is it *work* that we can learn to be grateful for?

And how can we thank you for holes of human folly—sink holes, ozone holes, bullet holes? Gratitude comes hard when we feel more anxious than hopeful, more cynical than wise, more distant than involved. We have so many more immediate cares and responsibilities, God. What good are these holes when we have no idea what one person can do about them? Did people of old feel the same way about the warnings of your prophets? Teach us how to respond to warning holes.

Most difficult of all, God, are holes in the heart: absence, loss, abandonment, death. These are chasms that swallow meaning and drain away joy. Can nothingness give birth to anything good? Can you, God, draw out from a vortex some new creation? A grave is a fearsome hole, God. Reassure us that it *is* merely a hole. Something must form its walls, set a limit, draw the circumference. We can only trust that this hole, too, is cradled in your being, sheltering as a womb. We can only trust that every void is but the birth canal for a whole new being.

God, help us to trust. Puncture our certainties, bore through our fears, clear the debris from the channels of our hearts. Breeze through the holes in our theories and philosophies. Sweep through the screen of our knowledge. Dig, blast, if need be, to open wells of wonder.

Thank you, God, for holes: holes that weep tears of joy as well as sadness, throats that sing praise as well as lament, pockets of wisdom as well as confusion, tunnels of faith through mountains of mystery. Let all the ambiguity of this pockmarked life make us gentle our words, extend a steadying hand, and stay our minds on you. We pray in the name of one whose wounds revealed your love incarnate. Amen.

Indicted

God, we are leery. We look at the lives of those who most faithfully follow Christ and give you thanks for their example. We look again and say, "Oh, you don't mean for *me* to be like that, too, do you?" We don't aspire to such intense devotion. And therein we stand indicted.

Maybe, God, it would be all right if we simply learned to love closer to home? Surely that is difficult enough for one ordinary life? To love the spouse who shouts in anger, the child who challenges us, the parent who keeps offering unwanted advice; to love the neighbor slyly prying, the inconsiderate colleague, the belligerent boss, the friend who betrays a confidence; to love the people whose lives are most intimately connected with ours seems impossible enough.

Do we really need to love the pompous conservative, the know-it-all liberal, the self-righteous moderate? Must we love the incompetent teacher, slippery lawyer, hypocritical minister, biased reporter, greedy developer, and loud-mouthed demagogue? To love even the lazy, the abusive, the dishonest, the intolerant? To love the people we love to hate? How are we to love, God, when indignation tastes more seductive than chocolate mousse?

God, have mercy upon us, we're not even sure we can honestly ask you to help us *want* to love some people. We are afraid (O God have mercy), we are deeply afraid that such love will take all the joy out of life.

And yet we hunger to love you and we hunger to love ourselves. Help us to recognize those same desires in others. Beneath the denials, behind the defenses, beyond the patina of worldly success or failure, may we find in each person a mirror to our struggling selves. Help us fulfill our deepest longings through inviting you to express your love in us.

We will then look once more at the lives of saints and give you truer thanks. Thank you for revealing yourself to us through their fears and their faith. Thank you for their witness to ways your loving-kindness overcomes evil. Thank you for showing us through them how possible, how freeing it can be to give oneself to love. Amen.

Jesus Wept

God of power and compassion, why must we grieve? We find that neither astute foresight nor careful preparation can defend us from all evil. Suffering makes end runs around every precaution we line up. No depth of faith, no strength of hope can preserve us from sorrow if even Jesus wept.

Sometimes, God, we try to wrap ourselves in familiar images of the darkest hours and dawn, of winter rest and spring growth, of death as only a prelude to life. Still, sobs overtake us, seizing, shaking, tearing all comfort into shreds. Tears will flow. Even Jesus wept.

Why this soul-heaving sadness, God, that assaults us at every loss of one we love? If we believe all is safe and in your care, why does joy flee and peace go into hiding? Why did even Jesus weep?

If you have made us for love, as we make harps for music, could you not have left out the strings of grief? Would the melody then not be just as sweet, the chords as complex? Surely rich, full strains of passion and compassion would delight your ears as much as ours? Ah, but sorrow is simply the breaking of a string, any string. If we are to love at all, if we are to make any sound at all, the fibers of our hearts must be strung and taut, as easily broken as plucked. And in your wisdom, you have decided that great sadness is not too high a price for love. So Jesus wept.

God, help us, also, to feel the surpassing worth of love. And if it is inevitable that we mourn as well, lift us up in your arms and tenderly cradle us through the storm. As grief runs its course, shield us from further harm. Preserve in us trust in your loving-kindness and faith in your mighty goodness even while our worst fears continue to rage and thunder around your feet. Then when the clouds clear and your glory lights up the sky, bursting upon our amazed and tear-stained faces, our gilded frames will shimmer in the light.

With this dawn of your grace, let us discover our hearts grown larger and freshly tuned for praise. O Resurrection, O Life, take these hearts into your hands and create such music that all the world must sing and dance for gladness. Amen.

Losers

Upside-down, inside-out God, sometimes we forget how absurdly fond you are of underdogs, runts, fools, and schlemiels.

We don't quite comprehend how you can enjoy the company of nobodies, the uneducated, whiners complaining of their minutest problems, the drunk pawing through trash bins; the runny-nosed fifth-grader with mismatched socks who can't read or add; the promiscuous fifteen-year-old, six months pregnant and out on the streets; the convict on death row. If you love losers so much, where is the incentive for us to work diligently, to be virtuous, to do our best? Sometimes, God, you make it hard for us to like you.

Gracious and holy, merciful and judging God, sometimes we are angry that you have allowed the world to get in such a mess. When justice is perverted and peace accords are abused, when food for hungry children is stolen by fat bureaucrats, when truth is derided and compassion sneered at, when beauty is destroyed in the name of progress and natural consequences are ignored for the sake of immediate gratification, where are you? Where are your prophets that spoke in the olden days? Where are the saints who once led the way? Have you abandoned us to make our own path through this chaos and confusion?

Sometimes, God, you make it hard for us to like you.

Almighty, vulnerable, sovereign, enfleshed God, sometimes we ache for prayers denied. When illness worsens and pain consumes all thought, when addiction undermines love and destroys families, when loneliness deepens and meaning has deserted life, when a loved one dies far too young, we wonder whether we may as well just give up. Are you capricious or impotent? Are you tempting us, testing us, punishing us, or ignoring us? When will you heal us? Where is our salvation? How long must we wait?

Sometimes, God, you make it very hard for us to like you.

And then the world tilts just so and the sky signals dawn. A bird whistles "Spring!" high and sweet and clear. Squirrels chase each other up, down, over, across. A child waves gaily on her way to school. There is life: tentative, brief, sweet, comic, tragic, confusing, mysterious life. Maybe, *maybe* you know what you are doing after all, God. And suddenly, impulsively, we decide to wave back, and to wave at the startled drunk in the alley, too.

Maybe we are, all of us, the losers you are in love with. Sometimes, *sometimes*, God, you make it very hard for us not to like you, love you, shout foolish praise to you, and surrender to your idea of salvation. Amen.

Offerings

What can we offer you, God? Shall we offer you our hopes and desires, our plans and goals? Shall we bring to you our fierce love and bleak emptiness? Will you accept the good we do even from mixed motives? Will you take the wrong we do in spite of knowing better? Will you accept such offerings because it is all of who we are? Look on us, God, and see the people you would have us become. Receive us in the name of Christ. Amen.

Open-handed, Big-hearted God

Open-handed, big-hearted God, sometimes your generosity confuses us. There are times we know great abundance in our lives. Our hearts overflow with gratitude for the golden health of ourselves and our loved ones. We luxuriate in the warm esteem of colleagues and the tender affection of family. Cupboards are full, there is plenty in the bank, and winter brings the promise of a glowing hearth, soft laughter, comforting words, visits with friends. We feel appreciated, our children make us proud. Isn't this what you meant for life to be, God? Our every breath can be an effortless sigh of thanksgiving to you.

What, then, are we to make of the times when it is not so? When troubles stalk us, is it because you, God, have turned away, been displeased, changed your mind? If we did not fully deserve good fortune, do we now deserve misfortune? When pain keeps us staring into the dark, night after night, when financial disaster looms, when trust is betrayed, when a child dies, where is your generosity then?

Or is it, God, that your giving runs harder, deeper? Shelving down like some granite ledge, backbone of islands, bedrock of mountains, shield on which continents rest, subfloor of oceans—always there, sometimes plainly visible at the surface, often hidden beneath gardens and meadows, woods and glaciers, seaweed, sand dunes, and swamps. Does your generosity continue far below simple beauty and ease, deeper than fear, standing unshaken by human failings or calamity?

Perhaps you give as the earth gives, as the sun gives, as the stars give, with a liberality quite unconnected to our strivings. Your strength and love and wisdom are just there—or here— above us, around us, beneath us, within us, all in such abundance that we cannot separate ourselves from it. It is as if, God, you cannot not give; you cannot withhold your abundance. Your giving is as universal, as evident, and as unseen as gravity.

But if so, does that make our living of no account? Are we beneficiaries of your goodness regardless of our actions or intentions or beliefs? What is the meaning, then, of human responsibility? That is what gnaws at us, God.

And do you sigh or smile or shake your head at such perversity?

"Wake up," you say.

"Listen," you say.

"See," you say.

"Your human responsibility is merely to enjoy me, to delight in me, to sing and dance with me through all eternity. Then you cannot help but live and laugh and confound the world with me." So you say. Then dear, open-handed, big-hearted God, what can we do but let the music flow? Take us where you will. Amen.

Seeking

God, life sometimes confounds us. In spite of all our learning and efforts to understand, there are times when meaning is flipped on its head. "How can these things be?" we ask. Grant us the grace to live into our questions, the courage to let go of worn-out truths, and the faith to trust that new truth will appear. Help our seeking to be more full of joy than anxiety and our living to be more full of gratitude than regret. Then we will know this time between now and not yet to be a rich blessing. All glory be to you, Spirit of life. Amen.

Testing

Do you test us, God? Do you look for us to prove our loyalty and love? Sometimes we can't help but wonder. When there are so many leaders nationally and internationally who appear to be only foolish or self-seeking, when good-hearted people are mocked and peace seekers are scorned, when fear perverts wisdom and greed slants justice, we look around and wonder what you are doing, God. Are you simply waiting?

When we observe the suffering of those we love, when all our resources and skill can do nothing to blunt their physical or emotional anguish, when our words ring hollow and repeated frustration drains our compassion, we find it easy to believe you have entirely abandoned us, God. Or worse, you are present and doing nothing. What are you waiting for?

When losses mount up in our lives—loss of work, loss of health, loss of safety, loss of love, loss of meaning; when disappointment stalks us and sorrow sets up camp on our doorstep; when we feel no longer capable of being moved by either beauty or horror, your waiting, God, seems like mere cruelty.

Or is your testing, God, as much of yourself as it is of us? Are you looking for ways to prove *your* loyalty and love? Are you waiting for nothing more than our openness to you? We would be open, God; only help our shuttered spirits, gently peel back the layers of clouds.

God, we would open ourselves to your love each day.

We would open ourselves to your healing each day.

We would open ourselves to your peace each day.

We would open ourselves to new life each day.

When appearances deceive us into despairing, remind us again that with you, O God, all things are possible. Amen.

CRIES OF FAITH

∞

Brooding Spirit

O Spirit who brooded over the void to bring all being to birth, we yearn to draw close to your mystery. As we are assaulted by news of horror after horror, of senseless cruelties on top of sordid injustices, we flee to you, bewildered, seeking sanctuary. What is the meaning of Zaire? Where is the sense in Ireland and Israel? Why Afghanistan? Who will show us the path of wisdom? Help us, O God.

Sometimes we are too paralyzed by shock even to know how to look for you. Sometimes we wonder whether you have abandoned us. Then gather us tenderly under your sheltering wings. There may we find a warmth that seeps into our tired bodies and spirits, bringing comfort and peace. If we are beset by worries, vague or all too real, allow us a time of refuge in soothing darkness to regain health and strength.

Sometimes in our fearfulness we need your encouragement rather than your comfort, God. We stand on the brink of the unknown and gaze longingly over our shoulders at the security of the good old days. If we stand so long that you must, for our own well-being, nudge us over the edge, let us know that you are with us still. Allow us to glimpse your presence swiftly winging between us and the abyss.

Shadow our paths, guiding, guarding, urging us on to new heights. Lure us with blue sky and sunlight, the severe beauty of stony crags and cliff tops. Teach us the patience of waiting out storms rather than struggling vainly into furious head winds. Show us how to find the currents that allow us to soar, spiraling heavenward to joy. Amen.

Fragments

God of peace and mercy, we bring to you all the jumbled complexities of our hearts, trusting you to sort through our doubts and dreams, our comfort and anxiety, our guilt, our needs, our longings, our joy. We lay before you the pieces of our lives, torn apart by mixed motives, by conflicting claims on our limited resources, by visions as enchanting and change-able as the images in a kaleidoscope. We come to you, O God, because we believe that you are able to refashion all these frag-ments into wholeness.

Do not turn away from us in our confusion, God. We need you. Although we may prefer understanding, we have greater need of faith. Although we desire happiness, we may need the discontent that stirs us to spiritual growth. Although we want to be right, we may need the humility that can often be learned only by being wrong. We want to be loved, but sometimes it is through feeling abandoned that we come to an awareness of the depth of your love for us. We dare not look too long or too far ahead on this journey to which you call us, God, or we might never have enough courage to take another step. We need a strength that often seems far beyond us; we come to you.

So we are here, empty and waiting and listening for the rus-tling of your Spirit.

And then, faintly perhaps, we catch the restless sounds of a new sense of purpose stirring, giving birth to a sturdy resolve. Someone has a need we can begin to answer. Someone has a hurt that can be eased by our hands. Someone who is lost can find a moment's rest in our company. Let no weariness or diffi-culty deter us, God, as we seek to travel with Christ into the realm of love. Amen.

God's Dwelling

How lovely is your dwelling place, O God!

Seated above towering storms, robed in darkness, draped with the suns and moons of a billion galaxies, you dwell in a great and high and holy beauty. You inhabit sky-ceiling rooms walled with mountains. You stride down sunset-canyoned cor-ridors. Lofty-columned, piney halls give green-scented shelter. Carpets of ocean waves, tundra moss, desert sand, and flowered prairies unroll beneath your feet. You have built yourself a house to make your splendor plain.

Then, God, how does it happen that you stoop to knock at our small doors? You, whose home is greater than the entire universe, you come to *us* seeking hospitality? What loveliness do you look for here? The fragrance of rain, the charm of butterflies, the play of otters, the music of wings are all yours—and what more besides? With all paradise and angel song around you, still you desire our rough-voiced company?

We are hugely honored; we are deeply dismayed. When you visit, you will notice cobwebs in the corners, dust along the bookshelves. You will catch us in petty complaints and sharp-edged anger. You will wonder at the ways we ignore persons and treasure things. You will be saddened by our unawareness and our anxiety. You will see and hear all this and more, and decide that this is no fit home for you and leave. That, at least, is what we would do. So, all in all, maybe it would be best if you simply stayed at home in your heavenly courts, visiting us occasionally, perhaps, in the beautiful temples, cathedrals, and bell-towered sanctuaries we have built for you; places where we can be, for a time, on our best behavior.

Only, we grow lonely for you, God: for your comforting presence, for your understanding, for your guidance, for your aliveness. Strangely, it seems that you are lonely for us, too. Or why would you keep on knocking? When we ignore you at the front door, you go around to the back. You are as insistent as a hungry child, as persistent as a peddler.

We are in a quandary. What you offer us is so enticing, and the price seems so very dear: everything of yours for everything of ours; all for all. We give you our home, our family, our selves, and you give us yours. Do we dare? Is it really worth it? No, yes, maybe. God, please don't give up on us. We are willing; only help our unwillingness.

Between our holding and our letting go, in the middle of our struggling and our yielding, begin, God, to make in these hearts of ours a home for yourself. Come in not as the stranger who makes repairs, nor as the guest who keeps hands off, but as the true and rightful owner. Clean, tear down, build, paint, decorate to suit your comfort, your eye for beauty, your purposes. Then maybe, maybe someday, you will welcome us into this small, cherished home and we will breathe in awe; truly, how lovely is your dwelling place, O God! Amen.

Grief

God of all comfort and hope, cradle all people everywhere who are feeling shattered by the loss of a loved one. Have mercy on all who feel deserted, abandoned, alone because mother or father, sister, brother, or life partner, child or friend has died.

Breathe gently across the empty, frozen fields swept bare by death. Break through the dull, leaden skies with a sign of your presence. Whisper to the wintry-hearted, "I am here; *I am* here." Do not add to their weight of sorrow doubts about your goodness, doubts about your love. Cup the cold void of their grief in your hands. Hold their hollow ache of absence close to your heart. Shelter their naked despair from arctic winds of terror and icy indifference.

Sing to them, God, tender songs of consolation, "All will be well; all will be well." Day by day, let the strengthening sunlight return to them hope. Night by night let friendly sleep restore to them peace. Soften the pain of winter with memories of spring. Scent the memories of spring with sweet gratitude.

God, we pray also for all of us who have been touched by others' feelings of grief. Sometimes their loss opens within us great chasms of fear. Sometimes the sense of our own limitations immobilizes us. Grant us courage to walk with them through the valley of the shadow of death. Guard us from offering glib words or too hasty assurances. Give us the grace to listen long and the wisdom to express our compassion in ways that feel caring to those who suffer. Let our inadequacies be vehicles for your grace.

Thank you, God, for the bonds of kinship, the ties of friendship, the links of shared humanity that connect us to each other.

Through the humility of sharing our burdens, help us come to a deeper sense of joy in our oneness. Through the stresses of suffering and the strains of hurt, bring us to a firmer commitment to compassion for each other. Through the examples of those who are practiced in the ways of faith, show us how, each day, to trust more fully in your power and your love at work within us, beyond us, and among us.

Then, dear God, bring us as one family to that fresh, green spring which no winter shall ever ravage. Amen.

Hard of Hearing

God, we know you call us, but how hard it is to hear you! Have mercy on us. Do not let this confession of our difficulty stand as an accusation against us. We are not deliberately inattentive. The errors that haunt us and the fears that plague us cause us to cover our ears and turn away. Will you speak harshly to us amid the hunger and poverty, the violence and indifference, the hurt and despair that live in our midst? How could we bear the sound of your judgment?

And yet, O God, we cannot bear the sound of your silence. Gently, gently pull our hands away from our ears. Softly pronounce our names again. Hush our complaints of ignorance, our sighs that we have no prophets left to point the way. Speak tenderly once more of your vast love for us. Perhaps we can quietly trust ourselves anew to your faithfulness. Amen.

Hear Us

Holy God, it is not difficult to come to you with prayers of gladness and thanksgiving when our lives are full of love and beauty and comfort. Our hearts overflow with gratitude and we walk in joy. We know ourselves to be your beloved children whom you graciously attend.

But when we lift our eyes to the world around us, sometimes our vision becomes clouded and our happiness dims. When we are accosted by one more story of killing or cruelty or degradation, when dogs bring home human bones, we cry out to you in confusion: Are there corners of the world that you have forsaken? When we angrily protest such violence, O God, let us know that you hear us. When we pray for justice and a sane peace, let us know that you hear us.

Sometimes it is our own small sphere that seems to be crumbling. When we stare sleeplessly at 3:00 A.M. shadows because we are in financial straits, or because a troubled child seems beyond our help, or because the pain of illness eats away at body and mind, O God, let us know that you hear us. When we weary of endlessly trying to deal with problems in our work or betrayal in a relationship, let us know that you hear us. When life seems to have lost its purpose, when loneliness, grief, boredom, restlessness, or some malaise for which we have no name is waging war on our spirit, O God, let us know that you hear us.

Hear our sobs and sighs and broken prayers. Hear our fearful silences. Take them into yourself as in Christ you took pain and death into yourself, to transform them in love. Enfold us completely within your Spirit as a mother gentles her crying child in her arms. Clear a space within us where we can hear again your quiet, persistent, persuasive voice. Surprise us with help from a corner in which we never thought to look.

And then, though it may still be night, in new hope and trust we can wait for your dawn. With new energy and life we can turn again to the work you have given us to do today. We can begin afresh to love you, to love our neighbors and to love ourselves. Amen.

River Flood

God, like a mighty river you surge through the dry and barren wilderness of our hearts. From our crumbling banks we gaze into your dark, rolling depths. We thirst, but here flows more watery power and mystery than we ever wanted or imagined. We hesitate until, too late, we find our feet being pulled out from under us. We struggle and thrash and cry out, God, why have you plunged us in so far over our heads?

You do not answer. You only carry us on, we know not where. You have given us one choice: to trust or not to trust you to bear us safely to a destination of peace and joy. Flow, holy God. You have made us and claimed us. Therefore we abandon ourselves to your grace and glory. Amen.

Too Good to Be True

Holy God, sometimes we are afraid to draw near to you. We know we have done things we should not have done, and left undone too many things we should have done. It is painful to admit that we are not the persons we want to be. Having had our imperfections pointed out so often by others, we are well acquainted with our weaknesses. If we now come to you we suspect that you, too, will demand that we do something to correct our flaws, and we are too experienced in failure to hope that we can change this late in the day. So why do you keep calling us, God? What, really, do you want with us?

Can it be that all you desire is to embrace us, shortcomings and all? Can it be that, whatever changes need to be made in us, *you* will make? That sounds so easy. We are torn between our hunger for easy answers and our distrust of anything that appears too good to be true.

And so, caught between our longing and our skepticism we stand at a distance until the hurt of isolation causes us involuntarily to cry out, "God, have mercy on us."

You answer with an acceptance so whole and deep that all fear and doubt fall away. For a while, at least, we live in the joy of freedom, in the freedom of intimacy, in the intimacy of gratitude. Your love has made us whole. Thanks be to you, O God.

In time we learn that wholeness is not a static condition, but liquid as a river, swirling, widening, strengthening. We discover that wholeness is your gift to us and not your demand from us. We find out that our need is new each morning and that there is no shame in that. And we discover that our own wholeness is inextricably tied up with the wholeness of those around us, the health of our community, the oneness of your creation.

Therefore, hear our prayers, O God, for ourselves and for all who stand far off. Amen.

Wordless Prayers

O God, sometimes we need you to hear our wordless prayers. Listen, we pray, to the beating of hearts, the sigh of air drawn into lungs, bodies' groans and crackings. Voiceless bones cry out to you and every nerve ending pleads for your grace.

Hear, we pray, the grief of the world: the soundless wails of the dead of Africa and the weeping of her motherless children. Hear the heavy grindings of injustice in Asia, in Central America, in all the corners where we fear to look. Hear, O God, and rain down mercy beyond what we can imagine.

Listen to the clamor and whine of the divisions within your church. Listen and forgive the self-righteous rancor for the sake of those who work to nourish and mend and heal this body of Christ. Hear the rumbling of walls being toppled by all the hidden faithful, speaking words of hope and compassion. Hear, O God, and draw us into the circle of your humble service.

Hear the longings of our planet: the ground which calls out for protection from wind and rain and sun, the rivers and seas struggling to cleanse themselves, the wandering refugees of every species who yearn for home. Hear, O God, and create meaning of our suffering.

And hear, too, the joy of the earth: the silent ripening of fruit and seed, the contented murmurs of suckling young, the uniting of life to life composing ever new harmonies.

Take all these wordless sounds into your being, God, and make of them a song of praise worthy of your glory. And in the singing of that song may all grief find release, all fear be stilled, and all gladness be compounded. Hear, O God, and rejoice in the goodness of your creation. Amen.

GRATITUDE AND PRAISE

Besieged

God, you surround us with beauty, laying siege to our senses. We can shut our eyes to cascades of color, cover our ears to ripples of sound, and still be haunted by the scent on a summer wind, be waylaid by the touch of rain. By a thousand strands you tie our bodies to this time, this earth. We praise you, God, for a home built of petals, wings, dust, and waves. Hear our prayers for those who feel cut off from beauty by grief or illness. May they be washed, soothed, rocked in tender glory until joy and health flow full and strong again.

God, you encompass us with mystery, confounding our minds. What we know to be right and good can seem as strong as granite or as elusive as the rainbow at storm's end. We are boxed in by deep darkness and blinding light, thick fog and empty sky. And yet it is our unknowing that makes room for new possibilities, our puzzlement that gives birth to creativity. Perhaps it is not we who ever hold the truth, but the truth that holds us. We praise you, God, for a home built of open windows and swinging doors, a moving floor and an endless roof. Hear our prayers for those who reject you from ignorance, arrogance, or despair. May they be lifted, carried, transported by wonder until every breath sighs praise to you.

God, you envelop us with love, eroding our fears. Through eyes that approve us, smiles that encourage us, hands that feed us, and arms that embrace us, we are schooled in trust, taught kindness. Letter by letter, word by word, you carve your vocabulary of grace into our hearts. What peace there is in knowing we are cared for; what joy in learning we have gifts to give others. Thank you, God, for a home built of family and teachers, healers and friends, singers, builders, growers, and neighbors. Hear our prayers for all who have been betrayed and abused by those they trusted. May they find a sanctuary of hope where they are believed and delighted in, where your faithfulness is given a face and a voice. Praise to you, O God, for all signs of love that enable us to risk the terror of mystery, all deeds of love that give meaning to beauty.

God, truly you surround us with yourself, gently, insistently inspiring body, mind, and soul to love you and others and self. We praise you for a home built on a foundation of church and scripture and the best that millions of people have offered you. Hear our prayers for ourselves, that we, too, may see the treasures we have within to give to you. We would be braided into the strands of courage and service, peace and joy that you are spinning, for the love of creation and to the glory of your name. Amen.

The Church

Thank you, God, for the church:
> for the prayers and sacrifices of the faithful who gathered in times past,
> for their appreciation of beauty and commitment to justice,
> for their learning and their teaching,
> for their endowment of wood, stone, and glass; stitchery, finances, art, and books, that your glory may continue to shine out from this place.

Thank you, God, for the church:
> for the speaking and hearing of your word in our midst,
> for music that transports us, study that enlightens us, service that deepens us, care that comforts us,
> for all gifts that augment each small giving, all voices that enlarge each note of praise, all spirits that strengthen each step of faith.

Thank you, God, for the church:
> for the welcome that requires no explanation,
> for the hard, simple expectation of honesty and kindness,
> for the invitation to contribute to a wide and holy vision,
> for the call to celebrate your love with all around us.

Thank you, God, for the church:
   for the people who show us the face of Christ,
   for spaces made peaceful and sacred by your Spirit's
      presence,
   for worship that clothes us with grief and joy and quiet
      blessing, marking us as heirs of your promise,
   for all the ways you continue to reveal yourself to us in this
      place.

Receive, O God, our spoken and unspoken gratitude, the up-
ward rush of our hearts, the glad overflow of our minds, the
high-arced flight of our souls' intentions. Hem our thanks with
the strong thread of courage and lay it as a mantle back upon
us. Then we will know once again your grace with us as we bear
the great and costly honor of embodying your love in this gathering called your church. Amen.

Far Horizons
All-seeing God, thank you for far horizons. Thank you for
distant vantage points from which we see the smallness of our
planet against a dark and dazzling universe. Thank you for views
of the connected, round, interwoven reality of all things. We
see a wholeness that is as fragile as a spiderweb and as sturdy as
forever, stretched and shining between your hands. Extend the
horizons of inward vision, too, we pray, so that all your peoples
can picture hope beyond impossibilities, find health hovering
around illness, perceive peace beneath despair, see life looming
over death.
   All-knowing God, thank you for the expansiveness of human
thought. Thank you for minds that transcend the limits of time
and space, making words, stories, music, images that arc from
century to century, continent to continent. Thank you for the
gifts of many cultures, the insights of other ages. Thank you for
all glimpses of truth, as unruly as fire, as composed as eternity,

your glowing fingerprints over the whole creation. Make our thinking more elastic, God; our certainties more permeable. May the wisdom of the past inform us without binding us. Let our present discoveries sit lightly in open hands, for we do not know what tomorrow will disclose. Help us to be honest in our reasoning and faithful in our decision-making, for how else can we understand ourselves? How else can we come to know you?

All-loving God, thank you for the breadth of human hearts. Thank you for compassion that identifies with the scorned, the suffering, the hardened, the arrogant, the frightened, the lost. Thank you for tenderness that recognizes our common vulnerability, for mercy that forgives our failings, for esteem that reveals a wider potential and a more enduring strength than we knew ourselves capable of. Thank you for the animating pulse of love, as fierce as pounding surf, as soft as nightfall, your breath flowing through the cosmos. Make our loving more cheerful, God; our giving more generous. Allow us to laugh a little more at ourselves, to cry a little more for others. There are times when we would love, and cannot. There are people we do not even wish to love. For your sake, God, for our own sakes, take our hearts in your hands. Knead out the stiffness. Let the leaven of your love work in us, stretch us, prove us. What you ask of us, help us to do.

Seeing, knowing, loving God, thank you for creating in us the desire to grow in wisdom and goodness. Defend us from distractions and lesser goals. When we fail to direct eyes and minds and hearts toward you, turn us aright. Grant that our seeing become knowledge, our knowledge turn to love, and our love emerge in deeds of justice and kindness, to our joy and your glory. Amen.

God of Laughter

Thank you, God, for seasoning our world with silliness and surprise. Thank you for barely suppressed giggles of children;

for chuckles at our own absurdity; for sidesplitting, teary-eyed laughter in recognition of the nonsense in life. A sip of your foolishness is sweeter than all the world's weary wisdom. A breath of your hope is more sustaining than all the world's proud cynicism. Thank you for each taste of the new heaven and the new earth where mourning and crying and pain are no more, but where all creation joins in glad celebration. Amen.

In Everything

Praise to you, O God of all. Praise to your creating, loving, holding, holy being. Praise for distant light. Praise for close mystery. Praise for raindrops, minutes, seeds, and words. Everything is ours. Everything is yours. In everything we sing, weep, whisper, breathe, Praise! Amen.

On Giving Thanks

Holy One, gracious God, we gather today as witnesses to your faithfulness. From of old you have led us, pursued us, guarded and prodded us. You have fed us with hope more sustaining than bread and supplied us with the milk of your loving-kindness. You made us, named us, called us to be your own. Therefore we come together to praise you and to offer you our thanks.

We thank you swiftly as the running deer, strongly as the rooted oak, sweetly as the scent of rain. We raise our thanks to star-high heaven and dig thanks down to bedrock depths. For you our gratitude is lark raptured, alpine brave, thunder loud, and bright as fire. And, too, our thanks comes cat shy, beetle dark, and mute as the tender swelling corn. Rich, round thanks be yours forever.

And yet, God, how can we truly thank you? Are you not the very source of our thanks? How do we say this glad outpouring of our hearts is for you when you are the cause of this joyous overflow? What can we give you that is ours to give?

We shall bring to you, God, our intentional choosing of that which is good. For you is the unbidden, compassionate act, for you the retort held in check, for you the word of forgiveness spoken, for you the enemy blessed. For you we seek the well-being of the stranger, for you we tell the truth in spite of shame or fear, for you we show calm trust in the midst of difficulties. How greatly you have honored us in this, that we may give to you a love unforced.

So, in love we bring our praise to you, God: praise though we rage, praise though we suffer, praise though disaster looms before us. For love of you we will try to endure the discomfort of a voyage beyond the safe and familiar. For love of you we will strive to be faithful to our promises. For love of you we will seek to make amends when we fail. For love of you we will dare to try again and yet again.

Then perhaps we will know our thanksgiving to be truly ours. Not alone for health or serenity, nor for ease and plenty, nor even for the care and esteem of family and friends do we give you our truest thanks, God, but because you have made us free to sing our love to you as long as we have life and breath.

Praise to you, most holy and gracious One. You alone are worthy of all praise. Praise to you now and forever. Amen.

Plain Gifts

Source of all goodness, sometimes we fail to appreciate how many are the gifts you've given us. It is easy to exclaim over the big, brightly wrapped packages, to say thank-you for feasts and sunsets and recovered health. Today we give you thanks as well for the plainer gifts: for bread and swelling buds and voices to speak each other's names. You surround us with compassion and beauty. You uphold us with a steadfast love made known to us in the life and death of Jesus Christ. Give us ears attuned to your voice and eyes to recognize abundant life, that we may live generously and link hands in peace. Amen.

Psalm of Joy

All praise to you, glorious God.

Let star-birthing nebulas and dying supernovas praise you.

Let burning suns, dark moons, and stately planets in their orbits praise you.

Let tundra frosts, equatorial rains, cloudy heights, salty depths, and every wind that from every quarter blows give praise to you.

Let every mossy, grassy, prickly, leafy green praise you.

Let every furry, feathery, leathery, scaly skin praise you.

Let microbes in their abundance and whales in their scarcity praise you.

Let everything that eats and is eaten praise your wondrous name.

Let all earth's peoples praise you.

Let old and newborn wrinkles praise you.

Let laughter, tears, whistles, yodels praise you.

Let pain nobly borne and suffering relieved, thoughts held in check and words kindly spoken, gentle fingers and callused palms praise you.

Let runner and bedfast, sought-out and solitary, wise and unlearned, broken and whole praise you.

Be praised, O God, by our songs and sighs and silences.

Be praised by our groans and cries and whispered thanks.

Be praised by soft glances and shining eyes, puzzled frowns and open wonder.

Be praised by all courageous first steps and last breaths.

Be praised by seventh, eighth, ninth tries.

Be praised by teaching, learning, building, healing, cleaning, serving, growing, and conserving.

Be praised with fountains, kites, wheels, and balls.

We hold out to you, God, all our moments: waking and sleeping, living and dying, loving and being loved. Take them and shape them to your praise. Wrap yourself in their glory. We will praise you always and forever if only you allow us the honor of bringing such praise to you.

O great and holy God, let it be the joy of all creation to praise you. Amen.

Rejoicing Together

O God, our God, for uncounted generations you have shown mercy and loving-kindness to your peoples. We have gathered here to rejoice together in all your goodness and to give thanks for your great providence.

And this is our pleasure: To praise you is like honey in our mouths, so sweet is it to sing of your glory. Like the taste of lush, ripened fruit is gratitude on our tongues.

We bring you thanks for the order and constancy of nature; for the beauty and bounty of the earth; for day and night, summer and winter, seedtime and harvest; for the lovely and varied abundance of every season. Thank you for all the comfort and fragrance of life, for the warmth of home and friendship, for the love and sympathy and goodwill of people everywhere.

Even when our days are steeped in uncertainty and our nights salted with tears, we will offer to you, O God, our prayers of thanksgiving, for never do you abandon us to sorrow or spurn our honest confusion.

Thank you for your gifts of patience and fortitude. The strength of your presence steadies our will and encourages us to wait attentively, alert to the impulse of your Spirit. You do not disappoint the trusting heart; your faithfulness sustains the anguished soul.

Thank you for your gifts of humor and hope. How often you catch us unawares and fill our bellies with laughter! How it pleases you to anoint us with gladness!

O God, many are the images and many the languages by which we name your goodness and power. Preserve us from all collective and individual arrogance which seeks to limit or control your love.

Thank you, God, for the skills and talents with which you have endowed each person for the good of all. Allow us to discover each day the joy of contributing to the well-being of the world. So may our deeds as well as our words declare our gratitude for your eternal graciousness and abiding peace. Amen.

Rest Stop

Thank you, God, for rescuing us from false feelings of security. Thank you for the times in which changes that we did not seek, or even want, brought us closer to you. If life seems to be a continuous journey, we are grateful for your companionship with us, and for the days you say, "Rest now. Allow me to take care of you. Tomorrow or the next day will be soon enough to travel on."

Thank you, too, for the company of others on the journey, for those who demonstrate a keener vision of your commonwealth or a surer faith when all sight is lacking; for those who push on ahead to light the way or slow their steps to lend a hand in support of us; for those who help us to laugh at our own foolishness or hold us when we cry in our pain.

Thank you for all stories of women and men and children who have loved you and served you according to the talents you have given them. Thank you for opportunities to use the gifts you have given us and for the encouragement we feel when others acknowledge such use. Tenderly teach us, God, to count all pleasure and sorrow, all sickness and health, all fame and misfortune as nothing next to the surpassing joy of loving you. Amen.

Singing God

Thank you, God, for your singing labor, creating and sustaining our world. Down into chaos your song descends, streaming trails of light. Up from the waters your music rises, giving birth to the land. You sound the notes of seaweed and fern; pine, banana, petunia, corn. You spin a melody of stars and planets, sun and moon. You sing into being penguins, dingoes, dolphins, and deer; spiders, sparrows, lizards, llamas, and humans.

And then, wonder of wonders, you give each one a voice of their very own in order to sing in harmony with you. Thank you, God, for such delight in your creation.

How, how can it be then, that we so often shut our ears to the sound of your singing? Our hymns fall flat, our caroling gives way to noisy jangles. We shout to make ourselves heard or retreat in panic to an arctic silence.

But you, gracious God, you have a gathering love; a wide-open heart; a warm, rich, persistent song that calls out to every lost and isolated one to come in; come in and listen again to your sweet serenade; come in to hear and to echo back to you your love song.

O God, what if our voices are creaky from disuse or hoarse from screaming? What if we have forgotten how to sing? What if others disdain our tune? What if those next to us are singing off-key?

You croon to us still, to leave behind the silence of shame, to let lapse the dissonance of grievances. You yearn simply to return to us our true voices and to hear us united once more in a great, jubilant chorus. Ah, God, the song of your desire breaks our hearts.

Thank you, God, for your singing labor, creating and sustaining our world. Down into the chaos of our hearts your song descends, streaming trails of light. Up from our throats your music rises, giving birth to love. You sound the notes of kindness and hope; justice, faith, courage, and peace. Keep helping us to sing with you, to sing in spite of the cacophony in the streets or in our heads; to sing out with delight in each other, in your creation, in you.

Praise, all praise to you, singing God. Amen.

The Unseen

Thank you God, for all things hidden, quiet, unperceived:
For winter life, asleep against the earth's black breast,
For back-of-the-eye beauty, ripening to timely birth,
For cat thought and fish speech and sparrow dream,
For hope curled softly in the core of every soul.

If you, too, flow dark beneath our consciousness, we will not protest. No, we will up anchor and push off into your streams. We may trust enough to pull in our oars or even, someday, cast them overboard altogether. Until we grow into the fullness of faith, God, let us have our little foolishness, our small securities, or we may lose our courage altogether. Only do not allow our childishness to bring destruction upon us or another. Carry us at last to the haven of your heart where all questions are silenced by love, and silence explodes into joy. Amen.

You Have Made Us

Praise to you, Holy God, praise and glory forevermore. You have made us seekers, longing for goodness and truth, gifted with reason and imagination. You have made us social, yearning for connection, endowed with empathy and language. You have blended us of earth and spirit, reveling in beauty, blessed with creativity. May our seeking, connecting, and celebrating honor you, all-wise and tender God. Amen.

GENERAL PRAYERS

∞

Awakening

God of all awakenings, we bring you thanks for the gift of another dawn and a new day. Thank you for the simple sensations of living—deep breaths, muscles stretching, the feel of water, the smell of soap, the comforting sounds of familiar routines, the first taste of food this day. Whether the night seemed too long or too brief, whether sleep was ragged or deeply restorative, you have carried us safely through the darkness to the ever-unfolding now.

Yet sometimes, O God, we would rather be asleep. When we wake to the awareness of a nagging anxiety or to the pain of fresh wounds a long way from healing, it is hard for us to greet the light with gladness. When we are troubled on behalf of a loved one or reeling from our own hurt, sleep, not awareness, seems by far the greater blessing. Do not wake us, God, without bringing us the gifts of faith and courage and the knowledge that you continue with us and for us. Remind us again that you are *always* at work to bring us good through every circumstance of life.

Sometimes, God, we would rather stay asleep because the new day feels already old upon our first conscious breath. There is no great problem to challenge us or goal to lure us, but simply another round to go on the 24-hour treadmill. We wonder mildly at our ability to get up yet again, to go through the motions, as we try to convince ourselves that things aren't really so bad. Life seemed more vivid in the dreams of sleep than in this state of stale consciousness. Do not wake us, God, without bringing us the gifts of persistence, patience, and hope that this winter of discontent is preparing us for spring surges of freshness and joy.

And sometimes, dear God, we would rather stay asleep because we want to escape from awareness of the world's vast suffering. We wake to news of yet more violence and death near and far, to accounts of disasters caused by indifferent nature or foolish humans, to stories of what is wrong with everything from the family to the federal government and every school, church, and political entity in between. How tempting it is to just draw the covers back over our heads. Do not wake us, God, without bringing us the gifts of wisdom, creativity, and love that draw us into communion with the many others who are listening for new insights and truth, who are speaking words of kindness and encouragement, and who are seeking ways to contribute to the well-being of all. Together let us be instruments of your grace and witnesses to your transforming power.

So may we learn to greet each new day with delight, eyes open to the wonder and beauty of everything that you are accomplishing in our midst. All praise to you, O God of all awakenings. Amen.

Be in Our Praying

There are times, God, when uncomposed prayers spring up unbidden from our depths. Whether these are ours or yours, we do not know. We only know that sometimes we cannot help our wordless, desperate pleading for relief from pain or sorrow. We only know that sometimes we cannot help bursting forth in noisy joy.

But in the long cool stretches of ordinary time, we need (oh, dear) a stronger nudge from you—you who are the source and end of all prayer. Unless your Spirit moves in us then, we can neither know your presence nor petition you for what is good. So we ask you, God, to be in our praying.

Be in our minds that we may rightly discern between narrow self-interest and a greater wisdom.

Be in our mouths that we may speak kindness and truth.

Be in our ears that we may hear new harmonies in the midst of discord.

Be in our eyes that we may recognize your fingerprints, still warm, over all creation.

Be in our fragile hearts that we may not fear each other's suffering, but draw close in warm compassion.
Be in our hands that we may work as we pray.
Be in our silence that we may learn gratitude for emptiness.
Amen.

Blending Voices

Holy One whom we adore, we know that you require no one special time or place to receive our prayers. The need is sometimes ours, however. In this space made sacred for us by the song and prayer, the music and words of your worshipers, we often find your Spirit brooding over us, lifting us, enticing us, comforting us, moving us.

Gracious One, you do not require the shouting of many voices to hear us; it is our faith that you respond to each solitary psalm offered from the heart. Yet it is in the hope of shared blessings that we come together here to blend the music of our lives.

Some bring here today the high keen of fresh loss, and some bear the deep, low throbs of loneliness. Some bring a lilting line of newborn joy. Some hold a sweet, sustained note of on-going gratitude for life's goodness. Melodies of sorrow, and descants of praise, the beat of passion and syncopated humor, discords of anger and grace notes of laughter, we dare to bring them all together here to you, O God, trusting that from our foolishness and misery, our stubbornness and hope and love, you will compose a hymn to the glory of your name.

Take the notes of others, as well, O creating, recreating Spirit. Make hymns of all your peoples' music: African chants, Latin rhythms, and Asian harmonics: ancient laments and modern improvisations; dance tunes, ballads, work songs, and lullabies. Open us to hear each other's music that we may learn anew that every woman's grief for her war-ravaged homeland is our grief; every man's anxiety for the well-being of his children is our anxiety; every lover's delight in the beauty of the beloved is our delight; every child's cry for comfort is our cry.

God, you have so fashioned us that none can sing more than one note at a time. In your wisdom you have allowed us each limitations so we must learn how to live in community if we are to live at all. We need reminding that this is not cause for frustration, but cause for celebration. We cannot do everything; we need not do everything. But guide us each moment into the one thing that is needful for us to do. Thank you for the people in our lives who hear the flat notes and have enough faith in us to support and encourage our better efforts. Help us to practice and practice and practice until we can sing the note that is ours to sing now.

Then by your grace, O God, may we swell the chorus that ever sings in ecstatic praise of your love and so reveal heaven among us. Amen.

Blessings

God of all blessings, teach us to bless our lives. Teach us to bless the past: to look back with gratitude for care and love, for homes and bread, for books, music, gardens, trees, sky, the world that gave us birth. God, bless the people who gave us life and the earth that sustained us.

Help us also to bless the hurts, errors, horrors, and betrayals. Bless the cutting words that cannot be unsaid, the meanness that cannot be undone. Let there be blessing to stop the hidden, interior bleeding away of life; to draw out the poison that gnaws on heart and bowels and brain. Teach us, patiently teach us, God, to bless those who have wounded us, and in the long, hard, aching reach to bless them, begin to know a deeper healing in ourselves.

Bless gain and loss, beauty and shame, kindness and indifference, joy and grief, for through it all you were with us, under us, and in us. Let the entire past be blessed as we release its tangled strands into your care and breathe freely again.

Teach us, God, to bless the future: to look forward with trust in your love and purpose. Bless the anxious insecurities, the fears of loss, the hungry yearnings, the dreams of wholeness and peace. Bless whatever may come so that in it and through it we may grow closer to you.

God, teach us to bless the present moment. Teach us how to bless the sensations of pain as well as pleasure, the feelings of sadness, anger, and boredom as well as happiness. Bless what we see and do not see, what we have and do not have. Bless light and shadow, insight and confusion, humble truths and ordinary words.

Bless neighbors and strangers, companions and competitors, the people we love and the people we can't stand, and all the people everywhere who are suffering.

Bless the roofs that shelter us, the fields that feed us, the communities that support us.

God, bless us again that we may know the serenity of a life that glorifies you and brings joy to your creation. Then, God may *you* be blessed and your name be praised forever. Amen.

Celebrating the Partial

O God, when wholeness is too large for our hearts and minds to encompass, we celebrate parts. One bird call, one whiff of cinnamon, one child's face, one word of love can set our spirits dancing. Help us not to dwell too heavily, however, on any single portion. Otherwise, we miss the wonder of yellow in longing for purple, we overlook the beauty of winter stars in our eagerness for summer nights, we ignore the salty truth in our taste for sweet knowledge. Give us the grace to treasure each slice of our world briefly, lightly, gratefully. Then shall we never be without awareness of your presence. Amen.

Common Things

Dear God, for all our adoration, we have merely common things to offer you: fragments of silence, bits of song, patches of generosity, pieces of prayer. We bring them tinged with doubt, frayed with worry, embroidered with hope and longing. Look kindly on these treasures from our hearts. Take them up in your hands and stitch them together. Pad our gifts with your love until they become an extraordinary quilt, giving warmth to all and praise to you. Amen.

Compassed About

All-encompassing God, thank you for enveloping the world in your grace. Thank you for wrapping the universe in cords of compassion that cannot be broken. Thank you for your ever-circling vigilance that marks the weary and frightened for your most tender care.

And still we fret, God. We lose wealth or time or friends, suffer pain or loneliness, feel angry or drained or superfluous. When we consequently turn in on ourselves, lay siege to our anxiety, God. Set up camp around the walls of our heart. Stop up the streams of despair that feed our sense of helplessness. Divert the flow of bitterness that feeds our isolation. Starve us of the addictions that feed our denial. Call out to us your terms of peace until we surrender ourselves to you.

Even then, we may continue to look longingly at the imagined security of our fortress. Although you promise us joy, we fear its cost, God. You say you are with us always and—do not be angry, God—we question whether that is enough. We know too much. We know that your presence does not make us immune to illness, bereavement, storm, or violence. We know that those who seek remedies for injustice are often mocked and hated. We know that no spiritual growth happens painlessly. Surely you understand how difficult it is for us to accept the terms of your realm?

Ah, God; you give us no other choice, do you? We give ourselves over to you or we remain captive to false realities. What we give to you, you keep; what we hold on to is forever lost. We choose to die or we are made to die. You drive a hard bargain, God.

So, enter into our choosing, we pray. If our yearning for you cools, help us yearn to yearn for you above all else. Counter our mistrust with your faithfulness. Surround our doubting with your confidence. Press in on us with your truth. Hem us in on every side until we can no more neglect you than forget to breathe. Enclose us in your goodness until we are again overcome with gratitude.

Thank you, God, for ringing us with people and stories that reveal your love. Thank you for encircling us with a power that brings blessing out of trouble and turns loss to gain. Thank you for swaddling death in new life. Thank you for clothing us in the peace of Christ which surpasses all our understanding. Thank you, God, that all is well. Amen.

Daily Fare
Thank you, God, for salting our lives with wonder. Thank you for moments of ecstasy that lift our hearts and give us wider perspectives on the world and your purposes. Yet we know our mortal frames are not made to live on glory alone. Compassion, faith, and work are our daily fare. Only help us to pass from hand to hand the joy that leavens our common bread. Amen.

Dance Partner
In this swaying, turning, slip-slide, gliding dance of life, O God, we are grateful that you invite us to be your partner. Whether we follow your lead poorly or well, whether we move awkwardly or smoothly, whether we even keep time, still you guide us, guard us, and keep us moving toward a more profound unity and a finer joy. Praise, praise to you, O dancing God. Amen.

Divine Carpentry
Creating God, complete in us what you have begun. We give back to you the raw timber of our lives, that you may build us into that which is lovely, useful, pleasing in all its parts. Saw, plane,

turn us on your lathe to expose the beauty of our grain. Cut and chisel until our various strengths and talents dovetail together. Fit us to each other: mahogany to maple, ebony to oak, cherry to chestnut, apple to ash. Sand, polish, wax us to perfection.

If we creak and complain, forgive us, God; we cannot always see what you are about. When the world's hard use brings gouges and stains, scratches and cracks, may they simply increase our worth in your eyes. Bear with us when we become discouraged. We look with deep dismay at the hatred and violence, the greed and suffering in our society. We look and wonder whether this humanity you are working with will ever come out right. As we contemplate our own fears, weaknesses, and failures, we cannot help asking, *do* you know what you're doing, God? Is this any way to build a temple?

Or can it be that our questionings and doubts are themselves signs of your Spirit at work in us—rebelling at injustice, protesting evil, longing for peace? Are these signs that you are not finished with our corner of your project? Then surely we, too, are not done with our work—the work of patience, endurance, faithfulness, and hope.

So carve away, God. Whittle, notch, file, and shape us. Then as you set in our midst the exquisite form of a new being, with fingers still curled and eyes unknowing, we think, yes, this endeavor of yours is worth being a part of. Perhaps even our flaws can be rendered beautiful under your hand. Therefore, finish us, God. Rub us with grace, seal us with love until our colors glow warm and rich with reflected glory. Amen.

Doors

Thank you, God, for the doors you open to us. Sometimes they are big, imposing front doors that swing wide on heavy hinges proclaiming, "Come in, honored guest; for you the feast is spread. We rejoice in your arrival." Sometimes it is a service door that opens to us. Through this portal we gladly bring the talents and abilities which are ours to contribute to the building of your commonwealth. There may be a cellar door into a dark, cool, earthy unknown that we'd rather not enter unless threatened by imminent storm. And sometimes there are back doors through which we enter your home as casually and carelessly as a child, with a cheerful bang behind us. Many are the doors through which you welcome us.

God, we have doors, too, but we are not always as eager as you are to open them. We often bolt and double-bolt our doors against what is strange or alien. We stand guard behind peepholes and chains. Have mercy on us, God, lest in our eagerness to lock out what is evil in the world, we unwittingly close ourselves off from much that is beautiful and good. Do not allow us to become so cautious that the hinges on our doors rust shut.

We pray for people grown angry or hopeless from too many doors slammed shut in their faces—those who, because of accent, skin color, sexual orientation, illness, disability, or poverty, are denied access to work, schooling, homes, or health care. May we together create openings in the walls of ignorance and prejudice, that every person may hear the voice of welcome.

We pray for people who are experiencing the loss of love or meaning in their lives. We know how well camouflaged a door can be, hidden behind a facade or a thick tangle of vines. Give those who grieve the faith to know a door exists, the courage to persist in searching, and friends who surround them with support and encouragement.

Thank you for all the people in our lives who have held doors open for us. We ask your blessing on the family members, teachers, friends, and mentors, the pioneers and pilgrims who have gone before us finding doors and propping them open for us who follow. Thank you for their wisdom and their love.

And when the times comes that the only door that stands open before us is death, help us, God, to see it *as* just a door, trusting that through this one, as through all others, you wait to receive us.

We bring these prayers in praise and gratitude for Jesus Christ, who likened himself to a doorway through whom we may come to experience your love and life in abundance. Amen.

Earthen Vessels

God, in ways mysterious to us, you have formed us from the elements of earth and water and air. You have fashioned us for pleasure and shaped us for community. Continue to turn us in your sure hands, smoothing out the nicks and rough spots, mending the hairline fractures and jagged cracks. If the stresses of life should break us utterly, then tenderly create us anew, teaching us through experience the meaning of resurrection. Amen.

Encounters

God, we hunger for encounters with the sacred. Let all beauty that delights our senses show forth your glory. Let all the truth our minds have discovered declare your praise. Let all the goodness our souls have met proclaim your loving faithfulness. Redeem our eyes from seeing without perceiving and our mouths from tasting without savoring, that we may worship you in wonder and wheel through each common day alive to mystery and miracle. Amen.

Every Big and Little Thing

You ask for so much, God; for time, possessions, hearts, lives. Do you wonder that we try to hold some things back? Lure us into that frame of mind and will where giving to you becomes our privilege and our honor, our freedom and our joy. Entwine your Spirit with our own until, with clear eyes and prodigal love, we offer you not less than everything. Amen.

Except That . . .

God of our heart and soul and mind and strength, we know that your desire is for us to give ourselves in love entirely to you, but it can be a difficult task.

We would give you all we own, except that our wealth represents our security.

We would give you our time, except there are so many things that seem to need our attention.

We would give you our anger, except that would leave us feeling so terribly vulnerable.

We would give you our burdens, except then we would have no claim on others sympathy.

We would give you our fears, except then we would have to live courageously.

We would give you our joy, except we are afraid we might never experience happiness again.

Therefore, God, we can only give you our "except thats" and offer our love to you piecemeal, as we are able. Please gather up our fragmented lives into your healing embrace. Allow our yearning for wholeness and integrity to overcome whatever barriers we have erected between ourselves and you. Help us to trust you more fully each day. Amen.

Focus

God of all mystery and knowledge, so often we see the world with eyes focused on shortcomings. Lead us, we pray, to a deeper appreciation of the beauty, power, and strength within all created beings. Reconnect us to the wisdom of the earth, the pervasiveness of your Spirit. Do not let the ebb and flow of our individual fears carry us beyond our trust in you. So may the words we pray join us together, filling us with fresh hope, courage, and resolve. Amen.

Forgetful

Wakeful, remembering God, have compassion on your forgetful, drowsy people. If we happen to begin a day without a pause for praise, intrude upon us in the warmth of the shower, between the lines of the morning paper, through our stoplight daydreaming. We are sad how easy it is for us to ignore you,

God. We are dismayed that we need your help not to forget you.

If we happen to end a day in exhausted sleep without a word of thanks, forgive us. Pull at the shadowy edges of our dreams until we puzzle over the piece of life that's missing and so once more become aware of our incompleteness apart from you.

And between waking and sleeping, help us to know the contentment of trusting in your love, the freedom of journeying in your light, and the surprise of meeting you again around each new bend in the road. Amen.

Fragile Lives

We come to you, God, seeking your wisdom for our indecision, your healing for our wounds, your compassion for our emptiness. Gently cup our fragile lives in your hands and breathe on us your fragrant grace. Hum to us a melody of hope until, giving a little shake, we are ready to stand upright again, spread our wings, and brave the changing winds. We shall then repeat your glad song to all the world as you give us will and voice and power. Amen.

Gateways

God, we allow so many thieves into our lives. We permit ourselves to be robbed by worry and anger, by envy and feelings of helplessness. Therefore, we come to you now with the prayer that you will turn us again toward that gate which opens out into abundant life, where no thief can steal or destroy.

Sometimes we need you to help us find the gate of faith. When grief lays siege to our hearts and despair crouches in the corners of our minds, lead us, O God, through the doorway of trust in you. Although the world is ever leaning into one disaster or another, although we may be threatened by illness or injustice or shattering loss, we yet can sing our assurance that all will be well, for your enduring love enfolds us. Help us, God, to trust.

Sometimes we need you to help us find the gate of gratitude. When we fail to earn the money or respect or affection we want, when we feel ignored or bored or burned out, usher us, O God, through the doorway of thanksgiving. There may we be awed by the treasures you have laid up for us: the pleasures of puppy fur or chocolate, mown grass, loon call or moonlight; the joys of singing or skipping or sharing a funny story or holding a child; the satisfactions of creating something new or returning something old to beauty and order; the delights of remembering past happiness and envisioning future possibilities; people who care for us, people who need us. Help us, God, to appreciate the richness of life.

Sometimes it is the gate of love we need your help to find. When we have been hurt or betrayed, when intolerance and greed have struck a reverberating hatred and bitterness within us, guide us through the doorway of compassion. God, this may be the hardest gate of all for us to go through, for it is too narrow to admit our bundles of certitude, too low to permit us to ride through on righteous indignation. Is it possible for us to protest the wrong *and* forgive the wrongdoer? Can we seek both justice and mercy? Only by your steady grace, God, can we safely evade the ravenous jaws of hatred without falling into the pit of apathy. Help us to sing with Jesus in forgiveness and passion.

And sometimes you show us that the way to abundant life is through the gate of praise. All laud and honor to you, wondrous God. All our wealth is of no account next to the bounty of your surpassing kindness. We can lay claim to nothing, yet everything is ours in heaped-up, overflowing profusion. God of wisdom and power, what shall we bring to you? God of mystery and majesty, how shall we proclaim your splendor? Loving God, beloved Christ, Spirit of love, take our hearts and minds, souls and strength; we lay all before you in glad adoration. Glory! Alleluia! Amen!

Gathered In

O God, through Jesus we know you as one who weeps, one who sheds tears for us and with us. You lament our willful unseeing and our stubborn desire for things that do not nourish us, for activities that bring no lasting satisfaction. We wander, lost, unable to hear your voice calling us home to you. Do not abandon us to our foolishness, God. We who cannot imagine any life beyond the labyrinth of our familiar frustrations and anxieties need you to break down the cherished, hated walls of anger and fear. Although sometimes we dimly sense that these walls imprison us, more often they feel like protection, and we do not know how to dismantle them ourselves. Therefore, by whatever means, O God, please pull them down—for our sake, for the sake of our neighbors, for your sake.

Break down the walls even over our protests, even though we cry out at feeling so unprotected, so vulnerable, so exposed. For then, perhaps, our eyes will be opened to your sheltering presence, our ears will be attuned to the sound of your falling tears, and our icy hearts will melt with compassion, and we will allow you to gather us in.

Enfolded deep within the downy warmth of your care, may we know a security that no storm can threaten. Within your soft tenderness may we find rest at last from our frantic scurrying to and fro. Here may we find there is shelter broad enough for all—all whom we love and even all whom we cannot love; all who are weary, ill, lonely, confused; the tear-stained, the war-stained, the enraged, the abused.

Huddling together may we recognize ourselves as your children, all having the same basic needs and potential, the same imprint of your image upon us. Help us to tell each other our stories of your goodness and power and beauty. Help us to teach our children, too, how to listen to you, walk with you, talk with you and enjoy you. Then shall your praise, O God, never cease from the earth and songs of your glory resound forever. Amen.

Gift of Prayer

Thank you, God, for your gift of prayer that refreshes our hearts, quiets our minds, and heals our bodies. We offer you now what faith we have, that you may deepen it; what hope we own, that you may direct it; what wisdom we claim, that you may refine it; what love we hold, that you may enlarge it. Strengthen in us the tender desire to be fully human and wholly yours. Amen.

Godly Sense

God, how do you enjoy all the beauty of the earth? Do you see yellow, smell rain, hear bells, taste chocolate, feel silk through the senses of your creatures? Do you experience our delight in shape and shadow, salt and song, skin and scent? Then may our eyes be honest and our ears attentive. May we be deliberate in our eating and tender in our touching. If your love comes to us through your faithful presence, may our love for you come through our willingness to live life to its fullest. Amen.

The Hard Way

(LUKE 15:11–32)

God, some of us must leave home in order to know the meaning of grace. Some of us must turn away from you before we can see the depths of your love. Have mercy on all of us who seem to learn best the hard way. Do not give up on us as we wander and stumble and fall into truth. Then, as morning breaks, do not allow our fears of you or of neighbors or of ourselves to keep us from your arms. Amen.

Have Mercy on Us

God of heaven's heights, God of inward mysteries, you are beyond our approach and too near for us to see. You are veiled in contradictions, revealed in paradox, ever moving, ever still, One and Now and Am. It is a dangerous thing to contemplate you, for it brings us face-to-face with our human limits. We might be paralyzed with awe, struck dumb by beauty, slain by truth, shattered by love. O God, have mercy on us.

Sometimes we are reluctant to open ourselves to you in prayer, for we do not always want what we know we need. We would ask you for greater faith, except that we know faith grows through testing. We would ask you for more patience, except we learn that patience is built by long waiting. We would pray for courage, except that would mean being willing to feel afraid. We would plead for increased wisdom, except we suspect wisdom grows only as we live through hardships. We would pray for a larger compassion, except that compassion walks hand in hand with suffering. O God, have mercy on us.

Sometimes we offer our prayers to you on behalf of others as a way to avoid our own difficulties. We pray for people who are hungry or homeless or oppressed without putting ourselves on the line to change systems that perpetuate injustice. We pray for those who are hurting because their suffering truly pains us, even as we turn away from the lessons that pain would teach. We ask that you enlighten others, while maintaining sweet oblivion to our own degree of unawareness. O God, have mercy on us.

When we cannot pray as we know we ought, then let your Spirit steal upon us with your strange, quickening leaps of life. We may have little desire to live faithfully, when that means risking comfort, security, or reputation. Yet we pray for you to begin to breathe that desire into us. We may be unwilling to place our time, energy, or resources at your service. Still, we pray that you seed such willingness in us. We may not want to love, when love demands humility, endurance, or change. But you, O God, can you not create in us a new heart which yearns above all to love? For you have sent forth your word of love, O God, and promised that it shall not return to you empty. Let it be our joy to be caught up in your trumpeting, tumbling, starry, wet spiral of love. Amen.

Held Close

(PSALM 46)

God, draw us down into your lap and hold us close. Croon softly, rock us slowly until the frantic rhythm of our hearts slows and steadies. You are with us; what will we fear? Your arm is about us; of whom shall we be afraid? The whole universe is yours; how can we lack for anything? We breathe in your warm fragrance, sigh, and release from our grasp all those things that lure us away from you. Yes, God, hold us close. Amen.

Holy Limits

How firmly, how tenderly, God, you crush our excuses. You take upon yourself our only human limits and reveal their power: the power of connection, the power of vision, the power of love. Through ordinary fingers, plain words, and simple faith you work your miracles of healing and justice. Let human flesh and bone and breath be joined to your Spirit so that we see once more how your glory enlivens all creation. Amen.

Home

Thank you, O God, for home—for that place which shelters body and soul. Thank you for the warm smells; the easy familiarity; the worn, soft, rounded edges; the cared-for safety and hum of the ordinary. Yet do not let us hide in comfortable gratitude from the suffering of those who have no home.

We pray for those who are housed in a building, yet have no house of peace; for those who have protection from snow and rain and wind, but no shelter from violence, neglect, or coldness of heart. We pray for those whose only roof is canvas or cardboard or the hulk of a car or a bridge overhead; for those whose closet is a locker at the bus depot; for those who taste shame in begging for help for the sake of their children. We pray for those whose homes have been condemned; for those who have been driven from their homes by natural disaster or the threat of disaster; for those who have been unwillingly up-rooted "for their own good." We pray for all who have fled from home before the mindless destruction of marauding soldiers, or the iron grip of a mad oppressor, or the cruel greed of a might-makes-right invader. Our heart goes out to those no longer allowed to draw water from the wells of their mothers and grand-fathers, nor sustenance from the land that gave them birth. And we grieve with those born wandering on alien ground or in camps walled with wire.

O, God how much easier it is to see and name such evil than to know how to counter injustice. Systems seem huge and fiercely complex, and we often feel powerless to sort right from wrong—let alone to act with any effectiveness. But how can we merely sit and wring our hands when individuals and whole cultures are being ground down and disappeared?

God, grant us this grace, we pray: do not allow us to become callused and indifferent to the pain of others. Hard as it may be for us to witness their sorrow, do not let us turn our backs. Even if it seems beyond us as individuals to make things right, still we can speak words of compassion to those who are hurting, issue words of challenge to those who harm. Remind us that if we would draw close to you, we will huddle with those who have nowhere to lay their heads.

And because we trust that with you, O God, all things are possible, we will persist in hope and humor and high spirits. Who knows? We may yet be surprised at the ways you can work through us to accomplish your purposes. We may yet know the joy of serving you more purely. We may yet comprehend that you alone are our one true and lasting home. Amen.

Hot Truth

God of sun-hot truth, chase away the cold shadows of our hearts. Disperse the foggy confusion in our minds and make our faces shine with simple gratitude. In a world cynical about generosity, in an age suspicious of faith, can we yet travel with you in open-handed trust? Yes, God, as your Spirit kindles our confidence and hope. Yes, God, as your Spirit cauterizes the wounds of our fears. Yes, God, as we find in each other the warm incarnation of your grace and love. Amen.

Impossibilities

God, sometimes you seem to ask the impossible of us. You ask us to acknowledge our weakness when we would rather show strength. You invite us to be strong where we are most aware of our limits. You call us to speak out when it is far more comfortable to remain silent, and you ask us to be silent when we are most convinced of the importance of our words. O God, help us to see that whatever you ask for, you also give. May your Spirit of faithfulness live in us so we can move through our days in peace and trust. Amen.

Imprudence

God, how often we rationalize our fears as prudence. Come wean us from the world's weary wisdom. Feed our incautious desires to be good. Make us foolish for love's sake. Weigh down our hearts with dangerous compassion. Then may we know what it means to be made in your image. Then may we taste the richness of life. Amen.

In Between

God, for much of our lives we travel in the misty between places. As we wheel between fear and exhilaration, as we thread our way between doubt and conviction, help us to fix our attention on you. When the way is dangerous, do not let us become so concerned for our own safety that we neglect to reach out a hand to another. Our hearts may beat to the rhythms of anxiety or courage, calm or excitement; only let them beat in praise to you. Amen.

It Is a Risk

God of grandeur and detail, in the power of your being you are far beyond us. All order and mystery, all spirit and matter, all time and eternity lie folded together within your hands. It is easy to fall down in awe before such mystery. It is easy to imagine how individual selves might be of little significance in the face of such transcendent glory.

But you do not let us off so simply. You tug on our sleeves like a small child. "Hey, what are you doing? I need you," you say.

In the form of a weeping grandmother you call to us, "Little ones, little ones, turn away from your indifference and your violence. Do you not know how precious you are?"

From the bed of a young man with AIDS you smile at us. "Ah, life is sweet. Life is very good," you say.

And we are confused. Could it be, O God, that we would rather sing of your glorious might than find you beside us in the thick of our daily fears and griefs and weariness? Lift us to a higher plane, we want to pray, above all these needling perplexities and pains.

But occasionally, we glimpse the idea that it is in the walled garden of our perplexities that you are working to produce fruit. Sometimes we catch you humming as you break up and fork over the hardened soil of our minds. Blithely, you scatter seed into the dark depths. "It will grow; if not this season, then perhaps the next; if not then, another year," you assure us.

But God, what do we do when, in the meantime, it hurts so much?

With gentle hands you smooth and pat the soil. Softly you tell us to be patient, to be brave, to have hope, to trust—whatever is most difficult for us. You say the world is not yet how *you* wish it to be either; still, can we not see how much beauty and grace and strength surround us? You ask us to open ourselves, to nourish the seeds within each of us, to weed out our petty desires so that we may be your people in the world.

God, we often doubt our adequacy for that task.

You say you'll risk it if we will.

No guarantees—except that you are God and you love us and you labor with us.

God, we just don't know . . . In our silence, speak to us, we pray.

God, we believe. Help our unbelief.

God, we are yours. Help our holding back.

God, we love you. Help our lack of love. Amen.

Justice and Peace

God of all possibility, we pray today for openings through which justice and peace can walk arm in arm.

How often nations seem caught in webs of fear and denial, hatred and arrogance. Too many of those who would draw back from confrontations find no place to go. Too many of those who would forgo revenge are themselves destroyed. Too many of those who would forgive have forgotten how. Too many of those who would speak boldly discover their voices muffled by self-interest. God, make an opening for true justice among all peoples.

We pray for the children of the earth, the ones who are the first to suffer from hunger and disease, from abuse and toxic lies, from absent or exhausted parents and a broken society that doesn't care. Surely, God, you are not impotent in the face of such evil? Make an opening—an opening large enough for all the children to see through, into your realm of loving possibility. Let them run before us down the bright road of justice and peace.

We pray, O God, for your church. Rescue it from worn-out phrases that no longer speak to empty souls. Shake it loose from tired patterns of behavior that wear people out. Free it from the self-serving norms of the cultures in which it is embedded. Set it alight once more with the fierce flame of your Spirit so that the world trembles with hope. Through it proclaim the power of your possibility for peace and justice.

And we pray, dear God, for ourselves. Forgive the foolish ways we tie ourselves up with impossibilities. Loosen the bonds of false perception. Undo the thongs of willful unawareness. Break the chains of helplessness. Breathe us into stillness, lightness, calm until we rest again in simple trust in you. Then may we set out, confident that you are opening possibilities ahead of us— possibilities of renewed purpose and higher joy, wider justice and deeper peace for your world, for the nations, for your children, for us. Amen.

Knotted Together

God, thank you for families, gatherings, encounters, parties, all the people with whom we share our lives. Sometimes, in the middle of muddling through, we forget how we need and care for each other. May the next misunderstanding, or flash of anger, or sense of betrayal only remind us of the depth of our connection. If hurt or grief weighs us down, help us to recognize that, deeper still, are the unbreakable cords of your love, knotting all hearts together into a commonwealth of peace. Amen.

Letting Go

God, sometimes we find it hard to let go.

With a mixture of love, wonder, and deep anxiety we release our children to the world: day care, first day of kindergarten, junior high school, college. We fear for their safety, worry that they will be hurt, and miss their smiles and hugs, their code words and inside jokes. We let them go because we know we must, because it's the best for them, because you have given them their own lives to live. Still, it's hard, God. Be with them as you have always been with us. Guard them, guide them, pour out your love upon them, we pray.

Sometimes, God, it is our expectations that we cling to. When hopes, dreams, long-laid plans crumble before our eyes we stand bewildered. We cry out, "Why?" We search for someone to blame, someone incompetent, inattentive, mean, evil. And yet our scorn makes us feel better only momentarily. Help us to move beyond disappointment, anger, and bitterness. Restore in us the trust that, whatever happens, you still have abundant blessings in store for us.

Harder yet, God, is when we must let go of a loved one who dies. We hold fast to our anger, guilt, and grief because any of them seem better than the empty, lost feeling of loneliness. We cry because the beauty, energy, life, and love that once was is now no more and we are, ourselves, forever changed. It is hard and slow and painful, God, both to remember and not let memory slay us. May your peace salve bruised minds, seep into wounded spirits, bind up broken hearts.

And sometimes it is our own life on earth that we must leave, God. We pray only that you not allow despair or fear to kill us first. Let us love and be loved to the very end of our days.

Do you, God, also find it difficult to let go? Are you ever tempted to renege on your gift of freedom? When we consider how humans abuse each other and creation, when we look at the hatred around the world, we wonder if you *have* let us go and forsaken us utterly. Yet if we have faith in anything, it is in your love for us and this earthly home of ours. How do you manage this trick of both loving deeply and allowing us to stumble, fall, learn, err, suffer, grow? How do you journey with us, God, and not collapse under all the hurt we cause and pain we feel?

Teach us how to extend this holiest hospitality to each other and ourselves. Teach us how to both love and let be. Teach us so that we may know the joy of Jesus Christ in all its fullness. Amen.

More or Less

God, we seek and wait and yearn for your presence—more or less. We want to serve you with pure and steadfast hearts—most of the time. We trust in your power and love as much as we think we can. Take our small, partial faith, we pray. Cup it in your hands, feed it with tinder, blow gently, steadily until we can no longer resist your holy desire and burst into bright flame. Make us beacons, God, along your road to justice and peace. Amen.

Mosaic

God, we would know life more fully. Wake us to a new day of sky and rivers, stone and leaves, earth and flesh. Give us ears to hear your many-voiced splendor and skin to feel your one-breathing Spirit. Break open our too-small truths. Help us to create from the shattered fragments a larger and more beautiful mosaic of meaning. May it be backed by faith, be framed in hope, and show the face of love. In the lines of that face may we recognize ourselves, our enemies, our liberator, Jesus Christ. Amen.

New Life

God, how amazing is your unending creativity, which keeps making what never was come to be. Every moment another thumbprint, a new voice, a novel thought is born, and the world is changed forever. Thank you for all the ways that supple minds and radiant bodies are unfolding your purpose. Take our rainbow-colored praise. Let it rise and dissolve and re-form afresh to condense joy and rain down new life. All thanks be to you, amazing God. Amen.

One Who Is

Ever-still, ever-moving God, you are darkness and light, beyond all and in all. You refuse to be named and demand to be recognized. We draw you as a finger describes a circle in water. We listen for you in the silence beneath sound. We feel your presence, as untouchable as gravity, as pervasive as space. How amazing that you who are formless have shown us the shape of truth; that you who are hidden have revealed to us the image of love. Honor and glory are forever yours. Amen.

Open Doors

God, how pleased we are by open doors. As we stand outside, they paint a picture of invitation, welcome, and warmth. Yet how fearful we are of open doors when we stand inside. They make us vulnerable, allowing the unknown to enter and the precious to leave. Help us to see you, God, standing in all doorways, as both host and guard. Then we can go out in glad confidence and come in to untroubled rest. Amen.

Ordinary Roads

Mostly, God, we do not live lives of high drama—of either unrelenting tragedy or unremitting ecstasy. Mostly we live in ordinary time, with ordinary anxieties, failures, and losses; ordinary achievements, pleasures, and comforts. Grant that we not lose our awareness of you and your great purposefulness in the midst of our ordinary busy-ness. To you we turn to find our core of calmness within the whirl of noisy distractions, our center of balance among a teetering array of choices, our heart of truth amid competing claims of rightness. Help us daily to grow more firm in our resolve to seek you, to love you, to walk with you on whatever road leads us to your commonwealth.

We ask this recognizing that although our energies and focus may waver, our trust is in Jesus Christ, whose passion and commitment to you was complete and without limit. Amen.

Realm of Heaven

O God, how large the realm of heaven is, broad enough to surround all reality, vast enough to contain all truth. Yet how tiny it is, like a pearl or a seed or a baby's toe—small enough to curl hidden behind a human eye. It is strong as wind and fragile as breath, obvious as spring and as easily overlooked as a blade of grass. How are we to find such a realm, God? Is it for this that you have given us seeking hearts and questioning minds, digging hands and wandering feet? Only do not let us search in vain, but lead us to the door that we will recognize as opening to home. Amen.

Recognition

One God, you are both revealed and hidden by words, music, and silence. You are both displayed and veiled by creation. We can recognize you only as we attend to the movement of your Spirit within us. May we love you enough to grant space and time to our seeking, trust you enough to wait with courage and hope, and enjoy you enough to endure our limitations with patience and humor. Amen.

Requests

God, we ask for your patience. After all these long years we are still getting to know you, still learning to trust you. We ask for your persistence, we who give up on ourselves so easily. And we ask—we dare ourselves to ask—for the privilege of showing your loving-kindness to the world. Amen.

Scent of Presence

God, your presence stirs us more than all the unnamed scents of ocean, garden, and forest. Envelop us in the fragrance of your love. Let its warm, sweet odor cling to us so that nothing can erase you from our minds—not sorrow or trouble, neither pleasure nor rage. May we be so bathed in your aroma that we leave a trail of love with every step we take. Then let the mingled bouquet of our deeds rise in a heady perfume of praise to you. Amen.

Search

Come, search our hearts, God. Look upon whatever pettiness or shame we try to hide; look with your eyes of love. Draw out the barbed stingers we would rather suffer in secret than reveal even to you. Seek for us, see in us, the wholehearted devotion for which we yearn. Uncover the wisdom and compassion we do not yet see. Search our hearts, God, for the living image of yourself in us. Amen.

Seeing Goodness

God, sometimes it is so easy to see everything that is wrong with our world. We have the impression that we are surrounded by violence, economic distress, political corruption, grave injustices, natural catastrophes. How does it all look to you, God? Is it as bad as our anxieties would have us believe? Worse? Or are we missing too much of the courage and kindness and loveliness around us?

Perhaps the brightness, the loudness, the enormous pain of wicked things draw too much of our attention away from the vast, serene background of goodness. Perhaps the intensity of our fear blots our the underlying sweetness and order you have established in the universe. If that is so, dear God, gently shake us awake. Give us eyes to see as you see, lest in our foolishness we attempt remedies that merely make things worse, lest in our righteous indignation we compound injustices, lest in our anxiety we aggravate the brokenness in our community.

For some of us, it is so easy to be critical of ourselves, of our loved ones, our neighbors, our leaders. We look at what is and imagine ways it could be better. We yearn for perfection since imperfection is so often a cause of suffering. Teach us to use our powers of discrimination and vision wisely. Help us to leaven our strivings for excellence with an enjoyment and appreciation of all the good there is.

O God, without denying the existence of much that is evil, we would celebrate and draw strength from the many more things that are beautiful and true. Without closing our eyes to what is hurtful in ourselves and others, we would more fully delight in the charms and virtues with which you have endowed each of us. God, lay siege to our disgruntlement with your great armies of joy. Amen.

Self and Other

God, we remember how Jesus asked his followers to pray for their enemies. We would often *like* to ask that you show some people the error of their ways; we are much more hesitant to ask that you show them how much they are loved. Grant that we may find you in the faces of those who are most difficult for us to appreciate so that we may learn humility when we are in danger of arrogance. Enable us to see you in ourselves so that we may learn assertion when we are in danger of overdependence. Engender in us enough insight into our own shadows that we may project neither our weaknesses nor our strengths onto others. Show us where we need to offer forgiveness for injuries we have suffered and where we need to seek forgiveness ourselves for harm we have done. Reassure us, loving God, that you are still continually at work in every relationship, in every community and city, in every nation and continent, creating new life and giving birth to justice and peace. Amen.

Signs

Thank you, God, for all signs of seeing: bright star, deep well, laughing eye. Thank you for all signs of hearing: thunder roll, wind sigh, calling voice. Thank you for all signs of feeling: water drop, feather stroke, cradling arm. You give us a world old with your presence and shining with life. Shyly, bravely, we step forth to name ourselves by your love. Amen.

Small Glories

Farseeing God, we are impressed with distance and vastness to the neglect of small glories. Bend our gaze closer to home. Teach us to marvel at wood grain, the color red, finger joints, words on a page, unison prayer. May we find you here at our level, in human time, breathing love into us, body and soul. How near, how holy, how achingly beautiful you are, O God. You have taken us; we are utterly yours. Amen.

Speak, God

(1 SAMUEL 3)

Thank you, God, for people with hearing hearts, who, catching the strains of peace, sing its lovely melody to us. Thank you for those who, swayed by the rhythm of justice, count out its mighty cadence for us. Thank you for all who, having forgotten the words to the song, still think to hum the refrain of compassion. Thank you for everyone who, though they haven't learned how to carry a tune themselves, yet recognize and applaud the music of truth.

You have not abandoned us, God. You have given us each other, and in each of us the yearning to manifest your Spirit. At the sound of your voice, let the dancers dance, the musicians play, the singers sing, the storytellers speak their tales. Let now the children run ahead and now the elders lead with clapping. Say what needs to be said, O God. Name what is wrong; name what is true. What one cannot bear alone, we will bear together. Do not let it be said by the hurting, the oppressed, the lonely, that your voice is silent in our land, in our time. Send forth your word. Pronounce your sentence of glory. It is a fearsome thing to be your people; an awesome responsibility to accept your love. Still, we have chosen to be here. We know no other hiding place. We dare to say to you, Speak, O God, for we, your servants, are listening. Amen.

Spirit in Us

Holy, living Spirit, breathe in us until your thoughts are our thoughts. Pray in us until your desires are our desires. Love in us until your work is our work. Play in us until your joy is our joy. Amen.

Stories

God of all truth, we are a story-loving people. Thank you for story-creators who have nourished us with humor, imagination, and insight. Thank you for story-tellers who preserve, translate, and elaborate tales afresh for each generation. Through stories, truth touches both our hearts and our minds.

And yet, God, we do not always tell ourselves stories that are truthful. Sometimes we become enamored of tales that feed our sense of privilege and self-importance. We know the attraction of stories that make us feel good but do nothing to nurture wisdom. We often prefer tales that lull us to sleep rather than those which bring us to a painful awareness. Help us discriminate between stories that imprison us and stories that set us free. Save us, too, from a sense of false modesty about our own stories. May we savor and share with each other the hard, honest, grace-filled lines of our lives.

We pray, God, for people whose stories are heavy with tragedy. Grant that the long-suffering peoples of Iraq and Bosnia, Rwanda and Algeria, North Korea and Tibet be sustained with a vision of hope for their children's future. May those whose lives are etched with illness and pain find you at work crowding the margins with love and peace. Breathe your warm presence into the empty silence of those who grieve.

God, there are so many horror stories of hate and violence and abuse. There are too many vacant tales of despair. How do we write new chapters of courage and survival, forgiveness and redemption for ourselves, our families, our communities? We bring to you, God, fragments of our stories that refuse to conform to the pattern of what life was supposed to be. Help us play with possibilities of acceptance and insight and new meaning.

Thank you, God, for all stories that deepen our faith in your compassionate power. Thank you for stories that sustain us in hope for the world. Thank you for stories that keep drawing our hearts to Christ. Their truth has formed, transformed, liberated, and delighted us. With joy we continue to tell and sing and enact these stories for each other, that generations to come may know your glory and declare your praise. Amen.

Strange Gifts

God, you know how much we dread feeling empty, lonely, weak, and lost. Yet through these vulnerable times you bless us with strange and wondrous gifts. Emptiness makes room for new insight and awareness. Loneliness links us to the yearning in others' hearts. Weakness prepares us to feel tenderness and true compassion. Lost, we come to the realization of how faithfully you pursue us. Give us the courage to accept such gifts, God, knowing they are wrappings for your love. Amen.

Surprises

God, you keep surprising us. When we think we have it all figured out, or when we think we will never figure anything out, you suddenly throw new light on our lives. What was once plain becomes ambiguous. What was once unclear comes sharply into focus. Teach us how to respond to these shifts lightheartedly, with humor, grace, and gratitude. Remind us that you are before us preparing the way, continually with us as companion and helper, and behind us as one who cherishes and safeguards the past. Thank you, God, for your unchanging faithfulness. Amen.

Threads of Life

All-wise and gracious God, we come together here today to keep faith with you. We come to express our love for you. We come to renew our confidence in you. There is so much in our world that awes and delights us, and there is so much that confounds and disturbs us. So we come both gratefully and hesitantly. We recognize that we ourselves knowingly and unknowingly contribute to both the glory and the mess that are around us.

Shall we lay before you the snarled threads of our lives? Are we able to trust that your fingers will loosen the knots and comb out the debris? Sometimes it's so difficult to stop tugging on our end. We are tempted to think that if only we grip tightly enough, we can avoid feeling any pain. If only we pull with enough force, we can control and protect those we love. God, you understand our anxieties. You know how much we fear being weak and vulnerable. Gently, gently induce us to let go so that you may do your work. Tenderly point out to us the confused tangles you are willing to unravel if only we have enough courage, enough hope, enough faith to give you our assent.

Thankfully, God, we receive back from your hands the strands made long and smooth and neatly coiled. With your guidance we turn to applying ourselves anew to that corner of the canvas you have set before us—running, looping, crossing, feathering, shading, laying down the colors of our lives so that your tapestry may be made rich and beautiful. We see with relief that we do not work alone. Thank you for all those who outline for us clear visions of justice and peace, wholeness and mercy. Thank you for those who give us the space and time and encouragement to do our best work. Thank you for those who forgive our lapses, understand our mistakes, and lovingly help us to make corrections. Thank you for those who have given unstintingly of their own glorious colors. We are startled and amazed; we laugh out loud at the unexpected joy found in giving ourselves. What were we so afraid of? Nothing, nothing at all can tear us from the fabric of your faithful love. Amen.

Truths and Lies

All-seeing and all-knowing God, we live in such confusing times. Our eyes and ears are assaulted daily by claims for this, that, or the other product. This program or that person is *the* answer to every problem. We are tempted to become cynical or weary or frustrated with it all. We hear cries of "Truth, truth here; lies, lies there; here a truth, there a lie"—everywhere a truthful lie.

Where is the prophet who speaks your truth to us, God? Is she among us, but we prefer to hide behind confusion because her words challenge us to do what we'd rather not? Does he speak to us from a culture so different from our own that we feel justified in discounting his words? Give us minds and hearts open to your Spirit of truth, that when it flowers among us we may recognize it aright. We acknowledge that we are ignorant of some things, but in our heart of hearts we secretly believe that our own ignorance is minuscule compared to that of anyone who differs with us. Forgive us, O God. Help us grant to all, no matter how petty or rancorous or self-centered they appear to us, some benefit of doubt, for much as we'd like to think otherwise, we know you care for them as much as you care for us, that you seek to transform them even as you seek to transform us—that, indeed, we may prove to be agents of each other's transformation.

And then, O God, bless us with a trustful serenity. In spite of the fear and hatred and greed that exist, your love is wise enough to preserve our world, strong enough to redeem our world, and sweet enough to satisfy every longing for joy. Amen.

Turning from Truth

Holy One, God of mercy, there are things we cannot bear to see. We turn away from the flaws in our character and the failures of our conduct. We avert our gaze from talents that lie buried and gifts that go wasted. We either struggle to deny or wallow in our imperfections. To descend into awareness, God, is a painful journey, but do not allow us to settle comfortably in a fool's paradise. Let us know that your Spirit travels with us, sees for us, and loves us with a faithfulness that defies our fears. Help us to keep moving toward the truth that sets us free. Amen.

Two Blessings

God, we ask of you two blessings: knowledge of how rich we are in beauty, talent, love; and recognition of how poor we are in faith, courage, kindness. Then, dear God, infuse both wealth and poverty with your Spirit. So may we grow rounded, whole, tangy, sweet—fit fruit for your harvest and ripe for joy. Amen.

Waking Up

God, gently wake us into glory. Accompany us through fears of loss; ease us through our anxiety over things strange and unfamiliar. You know how often we resist change, even change for the better, even when we ourselves do not recognize our resistance. Open our eyes to a broader vision. Give us hearts to trust your hidden power and purpose. Pool our strengths and skills to form a reservoir of hope from which all may draw. Then, when the morning is still and the world quiet, we may see in that pool the reflection of a glory greater than any of us could ever imagine. Amen.

Words

God, who speaks the world into being, we give you thanks for words. The words we hear, the words we speak, the words we read and write are the means by which we name ourselves, connect with each other, describe reality, and come to know you. Help us, therefore, to be careful with our words. Keep us aware of their power to build relationships or destroy reputations, to caress or to injure, to deceive or to reveal truth.

Sometimes we despair at the power of language to divide the world's peoples, to incite hatred and violence. When day after day the news of warfare drums on our ears, it seems as though our only choices are to live in fear or denial. We need your reminder, God, that language also has the power to disarm and to reconcile. Do not let words of sensationalism destroy our abilities to reason and empathize. May our leaders be those whose speech moves us to deeds of neighborliness and compassion. Give us the ears to hear those who are seeking justice and amity through fair talk and true speech.

Forgive us when we ourselves misuse the power of words. It is so easy to use words to protect our own vulnerabilities and expose another's, to vaunt our own character and denigrate another's. It is so easy to use words glibly and thoughtlessly simply to fill silence. Grant us a greater awareness of the ways our words create an atmosphere of respect or distrust, of anxiousness or serenity.

Perversely, how difficult it often is to speak the words we should: words of apology, words in defense of someone else, even words of gratitude or praise. And sometimes, when we deeply desire to speak fairly and kindly, the right words escape us. God, help us not to excuse ourselves, but to accept with humility our human limitations. Aid our continuing attempts to speak good words: words of comfort and hope, words of gentle confrontation, words of love. Help us also to learn forgiveness for those whose words have greatly wounded us, for those who failed to speak on our behalf, for those who misinterpreted our words for their own purposes.

Thank you, God, for written words that bridge centuries and continents with insight and truth, and especially for those words preserved for us as holy scripture. Thank you for the light shed by all those who have set down in words their experiences of you. When our own words seem unable to express what we want to say, how grateful we are to have the stories and poetry of others to articulate our doubts and convictions, our cries of anguish and our glimmers of hope. Most of all we praise you, God, for your Word made flesh, through whom you show us that nothing, nothing at all, can separate us from your love. Amen.